AN INTRODUCTION

TO THE

COPPER COINS

OF EUROPE

TILL 1892

BY

FRANK C. HIGGINS

Profusely illustrated; with many drawings by the Author from coins in his own collection

London

SWAN SONNENSCHEIN & CO
PATERNOSTER SQUARE

—

1892

And Reprinted by Spink & Son Limited
1970

One kreuzer of Francis Joseph I., Austria, 1851.

PREFACE.

THE author wishes to express, first his obligation to the comprehensive list of modern European copper coins compiled by his friend Mr. Lyman H. Low, and published as the Official Catalogue of the Scott Coin and Stamp Company of New York. The lines of this valuable list have been followed, as representing the most convenient order, and at the same time guaranteeing that the coins treated of might readily be found on application to this and other excellent concerns, both in England and abroad.

The filling in of the outline thus provided has been accomplished, however, by reference to the author's own large collection, from which many of the illustrations are made, and to the excellent private numismatic library of an indefatigable London amateur, Mr. Thomas Pocock. To both of the foregoing gentlemen many thanks are therefore rendered. To young collectors desirous of embracing the entire range of modern copper coins, the two volumes of this series, entitled *English Coins and Tokens*, by Llewelyn Jewett, F.S.A., and *Colonial Coins and Tokens*, by D. F. Howarth, F.S.A., will give, with but few exceptions, notably those of American and foreign colonial coins, a complete mastery of this most fascinating topic.

FRANK C. HIGGINS.

London.

CONTENTS.

1-1

AN INTRODUCTION

TO THE

COPPER COINS OF MODERN EUROPE.

INTRODUCTORY.

It will not be out of place to preface a work treating exclusively of *copper* coins, with a few words concerning the position occupied by that useful metal in the currency of nations, and the peculiar features which commend it to the attention of young collectors who, the writer at least, believes, will find the study of copper coins quite as interesting and more practical as a beginning in *Numismatics* than that of any other series. Copper and bronze, which latter is simply copper mixed with a certain proportion of tin or other alloy to render it of a hardness and fineness suitable to its employment for artistic purposes, have since the most primitive ages been accorded an intrinsic value which has secured their employment in matters of barter and exchange. Originally this value was real, because at an early period of the world's history, copper, tin, and malleable iron, were the sole metals with which mankind had become sufficiently acquainted to turn into weapons of war and implements of domestic utility. In the primitive ages, before the invention of coin, bronze served as currency by weight, or in the form of small implements such as were in common use, the same way as to-day knife blades and hatchet heads form the currency of the natives of some parts of Central Africa.

To the Romans, properly, belongs the credit of having first introduced a regular copper coinage. We owe our English word *pecuniary*, relating to a money consideration, to the fact that the Latin founders of Rome stamped or cast upon their huge pieces of copper the effigy of an ox. Hence the derivation from *pecus*, meaning cattle. From this humble beginning the copper coinage of Rome and of Greece developed and spread over the entire ancient world, so as to bequeath to us in the variety of nations, conditions, and types represented, an inestimable treasure of testimony to historical truths. The Imperial series of Roman bronzes stands to-day, in value, superior to the gold coin of its own or any other period.

With the decadence and extinction of the Roman Empire, the once all-important copper coinage of Europe dwindled and disappeared without leaving a trace beyond a few meaningless bits of metal coming, perhaps, from the wreck of the Byzantine Empire. The small values for which it passed in early times were for centuries represented throughout Europe by minute scales of silver, so mean and insignificant as to hardly deserve the distinction of being called coins, and which most frequently were told by weight. Then came a period during which the lesser fractional values were represented by *billon* coins, a base mixture of a very little silver with a great deal of copper, and not until the twelfth century did pure copper or bronze make its reappearance in Europe as a distinct coinage, while its use in other than the merest localities was restricted until several hundred years later. The middle of the fifteenth century may be fairly given as the period of the renaissance of European copper coinage.

The satisfaction to be derived by the collector from the fact that it is possible for him to reunite at slight expense a most creditable representation of almost every series which has appeared in the period intervening since that epoch, need not be dilated upon. The number of "curious" copper coins which have come to British shores in the pockets of her voyagers by sea and land, have counted up into the millions yearly ever since Britons have mingled freely with the outer world. There is no lack of hoards which the collector will encounter from time to time in divers places, and it only remains for him to select, classify, and study as becomes a true amateur. The home and colonial coinages of Great Britain, which of course deserve first attention, have been clearly and sensibly treated of in the two preceding volumes of this series, so that the contents of the present, its compiler hopes, will follow in pleasing natural sequence.

There are several points concerning the collection of coins which the collector, commencing, will soon find out for himself, after having committed a few errors of judgment, but which are well worth mentioning at the outset.

HINTS ON COLLECTING.

It does not do to go too fast at the beginning. The chief beauty of a collection lies in the number of actually perfect and undamaged specimens it contains, and a collection to possess any appreciable number of such coins must be the patient accumulation of a long period — nor is it wise to search out rarities in preference to all others. Rare issues are very high priced when in the hands of dealers, and are the field of the advanced collector, who buys coins as one would buy old plate and china, knowing where to sell again, at a pinch. The young collector will, if he keeps his eyes open and carefully identifies each piece coming into his possession, secure from time to time odd specimens which he could not buy in the open market for large sums. He should never lose sight of the fact that when he obtains a better specimen of a coin already in his possession, he must discard the latter, for which he may not readily find a purchaser. This should make him cautious about going to expense for a coin which he is not sure of retaining. If he acquires an indifferent specimen for a mere song, it may do to help fill a set with for a while, but it had better be left alone than over-paid for. Copper coins which have been long hoarded away, especially those of elaborate design, having a high relief, accumulate a great deal of dust and dirt which combines with the natural *verdigris* of the metal to discolour the piece and clog up every crevice. Ammonia or acid should not be employed to remove this, but the deposit may be loosened, without hurting the coin, by immersion in a strong solution of common soda in water, and cleared away by brushing out with a moderately hard brush. An old tooth brush is the best which could be recommended. The colour of the coin does not matter so long as it is clean, as old coins are all more or less oxidized. The surface of an uncirculated or proof coin should never be touched with the fingers, but the piece should be taken carefully and firmly by the opposite outer edges, between the thumb and index finger, as a damp finger-mark leaves an almost indelible stain.

It is a great mistake of the ignorant that only those coins are genuine which are more or less battered and show visible signs of age and wear. Coin collecting has been in vogue many hundred years, and old collections have brought down to our time plenty of very old pieces still in their mint freshness. Counterfeits of modern European copper coins do not exist in any great proportion, as the originals have not reached a degree of rarity to warrant their being profitable to unscrupulous persons. Copies of current copper coins have certainly been made at divers times in different countries to serve as tokens, but they are of such inferior execution, and badly struck on such thin planchets of copper, as to at once show what they are. Electrotypes of rare coins, or leaden copies washed with copper, may be detected by their failure to ring when balanced on the finger, and the excellent condition of such desirable coins as they will represent will at once lead to critical examination. Electrotyped counterfeits have each side manufactured separately, after which they are soldered together, An examination of the edges will detect this. It is a common trick of some coin dealers to improve the appearance of a worn and discoloured copper coin of value by giving it a bath of fresh copper. In this sort of coin the worn lettering and design will belie its apparent mint condition. The young collector will also do well to avoid the type of junk-shop dealer who has a few coins for sale about which he knows absolutely nothing, but which he invariably attempts to foist upon an inexperienced amateur at prices varying from five to fifty times their real value. A reputable coin or specimen dealer should alone be *relied* upon. Young collectors should endeavour to know others equally interested, so as to furnish each with an outlet for duplicate coins and exchange of experiences. The friendship of an advanced collector, and access to his cabinet for purpose of study, will be found invaluable if it can be commanded.

As I have already stated, a very few copper coins are extant which belong to an early period, subsequent to the final disappearance of the regular bronze coinage of the Roman and its successor, the Byzantine Empire. These belong principally to Italian provinces bordering upon the Mediterranean, such as Naples and Sicily, and are of such a nondescript order and so irregular in sequence that they do not furnish an adequate basis upon which to found a chronological account. They herefore will be touched upon in connection with their respective countries, which in turn will be covered in the order o their importance. Our work dealing with such an immense variety of types, it is necessary in many cases to depend on the personal aptitude of the collector, who, when a single coin of a series, differing one from another in many minor points, is described or pictured to him, will identify the others by important details unmistakably common to all.

As abbreviations constantly appear on coins too small to bear the entire inscription common to the series, the student will find it necessary to develop a familiarity with the latter, which will often prove of great aid. Dates given are those during which copper coins were issued.

FRANCE.

The first coinage of copper for use in modern France took place in the reign of Henry III. Le Blanc, in the quain French of his elaborate *Traité Historique des Monnoyes de France*, published at Amsterdam in 1692, says,—

"I shall not say anything about the billon moneys (of Henry III.) because they were the same as of the preceding reign. In 1575 were made Doubles-deniers Tournois and Deniers Tournois of fine copper. Up to that time there had been no pure copper money in France, but as now billon was lacking wherewith to manufacture Doubles and Deniers they were obliged to use copper to make these little coins, which they have always done since." The type of these first French copper coins was destined to endure upwards of one hundred years,

Fig. 1.—Reverse of Double Tournois. Henry IV., 1603.

during which a great variety appeared not only bearing the effigies of the Kings of France, but of a large number of their princely vassals in the provinces. The *obv.* of these pieces contained invariably a small bust of the monarch in the high collar or ruff of the period, facing right, within an inner circle, which is surrounded in turn by his titles. The *rev.* bore usually three fleur-de-lis in a circle surrounded by DOVBLE TOVRNOIS and date, or two fleur-de-lis in the case of the smaller coins, with DENIER TOVRNOIS and date. These pieces were multiplied by thousands, and are not rare. They are to be found of HENRI III. 1575–89; the Cardinal de Bourbon, pretender as CHARLES X. 1590–95; HENRI IIII. 1590–1610; LOVIS or LOYS XIII. (Louis) juvenile head, LOYS XIII. adult

FIG. 2.—Obverse of Double Tournois. Louis XIII. Adult head.

head and LUD(ovicus) XIII. undraped adult bust (latter facing left) 1611–43. The heads of course changing with advancing age. For Louis XIV. were struck, first Deniers and Doubles with a young head and L. XIIII. etc., and afterwards a series

FIG. 3.—Obverse of Liard. Louis XIV. (Young head.)

of Liards on the *obv.* of which was a crowned juvenile bust, titles and date, and on the *rev.* LIARD DE FRANCE, and three fleur-de-lis below. Later the Liard bore his well known adult head with flowing hair, uncrowned. There were also struck late in the reign of Louis XIV. pieces of two and four Deniers with bust, and six Deniers, bearing on *obv.* a triangular figure of three double l's (JL) crowned, with a fleur-de-lis at each angle, the whole surrounded by titles. *Rev.* a cross surrounded by SIX DENIERS DE FRANCE and date. The period of the foregoing was from 1648–1713. The copper coinage of Louis XV. was in Liards, Sous and half Sous, with bust and LUDOVICUS XV. DEI GRATIA on *obv.*, and on *rev.* the remainder of his titles and date surrounding the crowned arms of France. The dates are—first coinage, young head, 1719–23; second coinage, adult head, 1766–74. The first

FIG. 4.—Reverse of Sou. Louis XVI., 1785. (Type of Louis XV. also.

coins of the ill-fated Louis XVI., 1774–93, were a Liard, Sou and half Sou, precisely similar to those of his grandfather, whom he succeeded. On the destruction of the Bastille and subjugation of the king to the National Assembly, with which events the Revolution began, a new coinage was prepared and struck in both copper and brass, the values being two Sous, and three, six and twelve Deniers. The *obvs.* bear the draped bust of the King, who is styled LOUIS XVI., ROI DES FRANÇOIS, with date below bust. The *rev.* bears an upright *fasces* surmounted by a liberty cap and within a wreath of oak leaves,

FIG. 5.—Two Sous of Louis XVI., 1791. (National Assembly.)

while encircling this in turn appears LA NATION, LA LOI, LE ROI above, and L'AN—DE LA LIBERTÉ below. The value is expressed by a figure and letter in field.   Slight varieties exist, but the general type of these coins is always the same.

On the death of Louis XVI. by the guillotine, the coinage of the " Reign of Terror " commences, with pieces of $\frac{1}{2}$, one and two Sous in both copper and brass.   Their type is, *obv.*—a pair of scales surmounted by a liberty cap, and about which a wreath is entwined.   Above are the words LIBERTÉ EGALITÉ,

FIG. 6.—Obverse of Sou.   First Republic, 1793.   (Reign of Terror.

and below, the date, 1793, or a mint mark : the value is expressed within the wreath.   *Rev.*—a tablet surmounted by the All-seeing eye, and inscribed LES HOMMES SONT EGAUX DEVANT LA LOI.   To the left of the tablet is a bunch of grapes, and to the right a wisp of corn.   The inscription is REPUBLIQUE FRANÇOISE L'AN II.   In 1795, or the " year four of liberty " as the Republicans called it, the coinage was again changed. Pieces of five Centimes, and two Decimes were issued, bear-

FIG. 7.—Decime of First Republic.   Year 5.   (1796.)

ing the head of Liberty coiffed with a Phrygian bonnet and surrounded by REPUBLIQUE FRANÇAISE.   The *rev.* of the smaller piece bears 5 CENTIMES, L'AN 4, and that of the larger 2 DECIMES. This last piece was called in later, "UN" punched over the "2," and the final "S" obliterated.

The following year, however, larger planchets were used for the five Centime piece, while the Decime retained the altered size, and a one Centime piece was issued, which is very common and plentiful in France up to the present day, although it was soon discontinued. The dates will be L'AN 5–6–7–8–9. There are unhappily no French copper coins bearing the effigy of the great Napoleon, 1804–15. His reign is represented only by a Decime bearing a large "N" within a wreath, with value and date, 1808, on *rev*. Louis XVIII. struck no copper coins except siege pieces. Neither Charles X. nor Louis Philippe are represented except by colonial coins of the value of five and ten Centimes, which bear beautiful busts. These circulated freely at home, and are common. On the overthrow of Louis Philippe and establishment of the second Republic with Prince Louis Napoleon Bonaparte as President, the one-Centime piece of the first Republic was revived from the original *obv*. dies, and given a *rev*. differing only in the substitution of the dates, 1848–49–50 and 51 for the Republican year. The Prince-President on becoming Napoleon III. issued fine bronze pieces of one, two, five and ten Centimes, bearing his head within a circle of dots, and the legend NAPOLEON III.

FIG. 8.—Ten Centimes of Napoleon III., 1855.

EMPEREUR, with date under bust, 1852–57. *Rev.*—the Imperial eagle perched upon a thunderbolt within circle of dots, EMPIRE FRANÇAIS above, and value UN, DEUX, CINQ or DIX CENTIMES below. These are still the most common type current in France to-day. In 1861 a new bust of the Emperor was substituted with a crown of laurel, referring to his victory at the battle of Magenta, and the, since famous, waxed moustache. Dates of the latter issue 1861 to 1865.

The coins of the present Republic are precisely similar in size, appearance and value, but the head of the Emperor has given place to one of Ceres, and the legend REPUBLIQUE

FIG. 9.—Ten Centimes of the "Third Republic," 1870–

FRANÇAISE, with date below. On the *rev.* the value, 1, 2, 5, or 10 CENTIMES within a wreath of olive and laurel, surrounded by the text of modern France, LIBERTÉ*EGALITÉ*FRATERNITÉ.

FRENCH PROVINCIAL ISSUES.

It has been noted that the little *Doubles* and *Deniers Tournois* were not only multiplied by the Kings themselves in France, but imitated by princely vassals and the governors of distant provinces. The general appearance of the original coin is always preserved, and in most cases the *rev.* type with the fleur-de-lis is unaltered. We meet, however, with "*Doubles de Lorraine,*" "*Liards de Bouillon,*" etc., only departing from the series in matter of lettering and minor details, and others on which the arms of their issuers appear. The following is a list of the principal series and types of provincial issue which will be met with.

BOUILLON.—*Double Tournois* of Duke William Robert, with bust, 1587.

BOUILLON and SEDAN.—*Double Tournois. Obv.*—Bust of Henry de la Tour. *Rev.*—Arms and value, 1568–1614, also varieties of *Liards*, with bust, date and titles on *obv.*, and arms on *rev.* Latterly one with crowned H; dates, 1613–14–15.

Doubles Tournois with busts, F. Maurice, 1632–3, Godf(rey) Maurice, 1636–40; also *Liard*, 1681, with arms only on *Obv.*

FIG. 10.—Double Tournois of F. Maurice of Bouillon, 1632.

BURGUNDY.—*Liards.* Philip II. (of Spain), 1559–1588. Albert and Elizabeth, 1616. Philip IV. (of Spain), 1636–65, and additional type of a crowned mantle answering for rulers from 1665 to 1752.

CHATEAU-RENAUD.—*Doubles Tournois.* Bust and title

FIG. 11.—Double Tournois of F. de Bourbon, Prince of Conti, 1613. Chateau Renaud.

of F. de Bourbon (François) Prince de Conti, 1613–14. *Liard*, with crowned arms, and titles, 1614.

CUGNON.—*Double Tournois.* John Theodore, 1634. *Denier.* Ferdinand Charles, 1655; *rev.* of latter, three roses or four fleur-de-lis.

DOMBES.—*Doubles Tournois* of Louis, 1582; Francis,

FIG. 12.— Obverse of Double Tournois. Marie of Dombes, 1619–28.

1585–89; Henry, 1595; Maria, 1619–28. There are two types of the foregoing. One with bust as usual, and other with simple initial crowned. *Doubles* and *Deniers Tournois* of Gaston d'Orleans, 1649–52, and *Liards* of Anna Maria Louisa, 1673, the latter bearing a crowned M (a tiny coin, often clipped).

HENRICHMONT.—*Doubles Tournois* of Max de Bethune, 1597–1641, and Max Francis de Bethune, 1641–61. The arms on *rev.* consist of circle of eight fleur-de-lis encircling shield.

LORRAINE.—*Doubles de Lorraine*, Louis XIII., type of royal issues. *Liards* of Leopold, 1706–28.

MONTBELIARD.—*Doubles Tournois*, Louis XIII., 1638. *Liards* of Leopold Eberhard, D.W.M., 1710–15.

NEVERS.—*Deniers* and *Doubles Tournois* and *Liards* of Charles de Gonzaga, 1601–37.   (Bust and Arms.)

ORANGE (ARAUSIO, ORASICA).—*Doubles Tournois*, Frederick Henry (FRED. HENR. D.G. PRI. AV.), 1636–46. *Deniers Tournois* of William Henry, 1650–4.

PFALZBURG and LIXHEIM.—*Doubles Tournois* of Louis XIII., 1633–3.

STRASBURG.—Both Louis XVIII. and Napoleon I. here issued *Decimes* in 1815, bearing a crowned "L" or "N" within wreath, with value and date on *rev.*

With reference to the isolated letters which appear on almost all French coins as mint-marks, the following list will prove instructive.   A. Paris; A. A. Metz; B. Rouen; BB. Strasburg; C. St. Lo; D. Lyons; E. Tours; F. Angers; G. Poitiers; G. and lion, Geneva; H. La Rochelle; I. Limoges; K. Bordeaux; L. Bayonne; M. Toulouse; M. A. Marseilles; N. Montpelier; P. Dijon; Q. Chalons; R. Orleans; S. Troyes; T. Nantes; W. Lille; X. Ville-franche; Y. Bourges; Z. Dauphiné; &, Aix; a cow, Pau; *g*, Bretagne.

SPAIN.

The transition from small pieces of base silver to larger coins of copper and bronze to represent the same values seems to have taken place in Spain early in the reign of Ferdinand and Isabella, at which time coins of those metals again began to be common in the South of Europe. The King of Arragon at this epoch was also King of Naples and Sicily, which states had always preserved a limited copper coinage. After the overthrow of the Byzantine rule in Naples by the Normans, the latter continued the issue of copper which they found in vogue, as did successively the German and Arragonese princes, bringing it to the time of Ferdinand I., who *definitely* introduced it into his Spanish dominions. Base silver had already become so bad in all Spain that commerce was nearly ruined by it, and specimens of the coinage before the time of Ferdinand seem almost pure copper ; but they were not legally so, and so escape being made subjects of our narrative. The coins of Spain almost invariably bear the Lion and Castle, by which they may be readily identified. The earlier copper coins have the Castle on the *obv.* and Lion on the *rev.*, each in a cartouche or shield, surrounded by part of the inscription. Those of Ferdinand of Arragon and Isabella of Castille and Leon united, 1474–1804, bear FERDINANDVS · ET · ELISABET ·

FIG. 13.—Obverse of Eight Maravedis.   Ferdinand and Isabella, 1474–1504.

on *obv.*, and CAS · LE · REX · ET · REGINA on *rev.* There are several copper coins of Ferdinand alone which bear a Gothic initial " F " on *obv.* The values expressed are *Octavos*, *Cuartos*, and *Double Cuartos*. The minority of Charles I., the eldest grandson of Ferdinand and Isabella, during which his mother

Joanna, the actual Queen of Castille, was hopelessly demented, is represented by a copper *Cuarto*, having a " Y " on the *obv.* and the crowned pillars of Hercules on the *rev.* Dates, 1516–20. Charles I. alone (he became later the great Charles V. of Germany) issued a Cuarto and Double Cuarto, with the Castle and Lion *obv.* and *rev.* respectively. Title, CAROLVS . D . G . HISPANIARVM . REX. Dates, 1520–1556. ˉ Philip II. issued from 1556 to 1598 pieces of two, four and eight Maravedis of the Castle and Lion type, with the values in the field. Title, PHILIPPUS II, HISP(aniarum) REX.

Philip III. coined values of one, two, four and eight Maravedis. The one Maravedi bore his monogram crowned, and the rest the Castle and Lion. Of the three larger pieces there are two types : one has the arms upon crowned shields with the inscription around Lion on *rev.* HISPAN(iarum) · REX · and the date in field, while the other bears the arms in ornamented cartouches, while he is styled HISPAN · REGNORVM ·

FIG. 14.—Eight Maravedis of Philip III., 1602.

REX with date following. The dates run from 1598 to 1612. Of Philip IV. there is a scarce 8 Maravedis of 1622, like those of the preceding reign ; but his regular coinages were excessively ugly coins of 4, 8, and 16 Maravedis value, bearing bust and titles on one side, and a crowned shield of complicated arms on the *rev.* The workmanship of these coins is very crude, and the engraving looks more like the efforts of amateur die-sinkers than of artists. The coins all resemble each other, but the different heads or rather caricatures of Philip IV. are innumerable. The dates are all in the latter part of his reign, 1660–65.

The issue, however, seems to have been insufficient, as the old copper coinage, was repeatedly called in and counterstamped with new dates and ever-decreasing values. These pieces exist in great numbers, and are sometimes very puzzling, as their surface presents a mass of battered remnants of the original design and the later additions. Pieces are punched successively with XII, VIII, and VI, with a new date for each

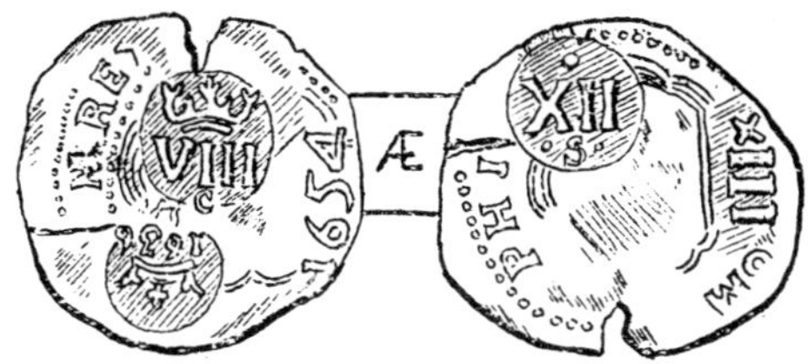

Fig. 15.—Counterstamped Eight Maravedis of Philip II., with value raised and lowered in reign of Philip IV.

counterstamp, and so on. This was called for by the constant clipping which went on ; for however little profit could be extracted from a clipped copper coin, there seemed to have been individuals who thought it worth their while to damage them.

Of Charles II. we have only two pieces of two Maravedis value, both of which are scarce. The first struck from 1680 to 95 are thick, mis-shapen pieces of copper, much clipped. They bear the Spanish arms and II on *obv.* and a lion on *rev.* The second type bears a rude bust, and on *rev.* a monogram C C II.

With Philip V. the copper coinage of Spain again becomes attractive and artistic. Instead of the Lion and Castle on

Fig. 16.—Four Maravedis of Philip V., 1719.

opposite sides we have from now on, the full Spanish coat-of-arms always occupying the *rev.* The Castle and Lion together with the *fleur de-lis* of the French Bourbons, from whom this Philip sprung.   He issued in copper pieces of 1, 2, 3, 4, and 6 Maravedis of several types.   Several of the earlier issues may be recognised by large crowned "v"s, the value generally expressed within.   The best and commonest type, however, has on *obv.* a Lion, crowned and seated, holding sword and sceptre, and guarding two globes.   The legend is VTRUMQ + VIRT + PROTEGO, date following.   Dates, 1710–46.

During the reign of Ferdinand VI., 1746–59, coins of 1 and 2 Maravedis were issued of the same type as the preceding. With Charles III. in 1772 we have the commencement of an issue of pieces of 1, 2, 4, and 8 Maravedis of a type which continued, with merely changes of *obv.*, as new rulers appeared, until 1833.   The *obv.* presents the head of the king sur-

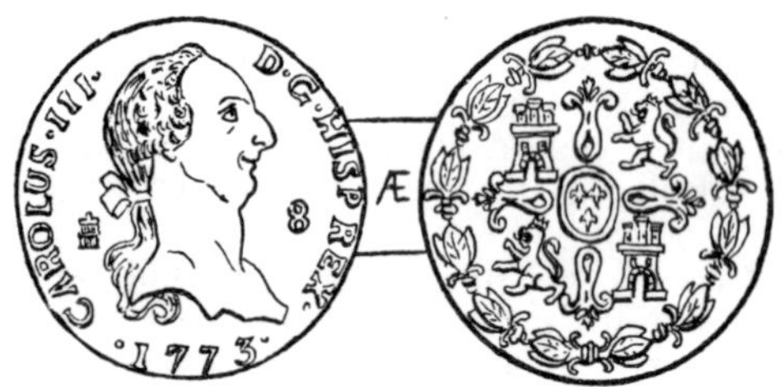

FIG. 17.—Eight Maravedis of Charles III., 1773.

rounded by his name and title of D · G · HISP · (aniarum) REX · and date.

CAROLUS III, 1772–88 ; CAROLVS IIII (or IV), 1788–1808 ; JOSEPHUS · NAP · (oleon), 1808–13 ; and FERDIN · (andus) VII (or 7°), 1808–33.   The *rev.* consists of the arms of Spain, quartered by an ornamental cross, of which the centre is an oval containing the three Bourbon *fleur-de-lis*, the whole surrounded by a wreath.   There are various *obv.* of the coins of Ferdinand VII.   They bear a small bare head from 1813 to 1816, a small laureated head from 1817 to 1824, a large bare head from 1824 to 1827, and a large laureated head from 1827 to 1833.   On the accession of Ferdinand's daughter, Isabella II., in 1833, the foregoing type was slightly changed by reason of the length of her title, which continued from the *obv.* to the *rev.*, where it displaced the wreath.   In full it reads ISABEL 2ᴬ POR LA G · (racia) DE · DIOS Y LA CONST · (itucion)—

REYNA DE LAS ESPAÑAS. This type in 1, 2, 4 and 8 Maravedis continues until 1858. A variety of the 8 Maravedis of 1835-6 has the value on *rev*.

FIG. 18.—Eight Maravedis of Ferdinand VII. (large laureated head), 1830.

The first deviation was a Medio ($\frac{1}{2}$) Real struck in 1848.

Then came a very handsome set of decimal parts of a Real struck from 1850 to 1853. They bear on *obv*. crowned arms on shields of a new and elaborate pattern, with usual inscription surrounding. The centre of the *rev*. is occupied by the value from "Medio Real" to "Media Decima de Real," four pieces in all. The value is surmounted by a tiny wreath, and the whole enclosed in a circle of buds, outside of which is the continuation of title from *obv*. The series of "Centimos de Real" run from 1854 to 1864. They bear a very plump and pretty portrait of Queen Isabella, surrounded by titles, with date below bust. On the *rev*., arms crowned in midst of

FIG. 19.—Five Centimos "de Escudo" of Isabella II., 1867

wreath; above, REYNA DE ESPAÑA; below, 5, 10 or 25 CENT (imos) DE REAL. These are the last *Copper* coins. In 1866 began the *Bronze* coinage of "Centimos de Escudo," values

$\frac{1}{2}$, 1, 2$\frac{1}{2}$, and 5.   These are much larger. in proportion than the coins of the series preceding them, have a slightly older head within a circle of pellets, and the arms on *rev.* are in crowned oval in circle of pellets instead of shield.   The value is expressed below.   Last issue 1868.   The 1, 2, 5 and 10 Centimos of the Republic which followed have : *Obv.*—a Lion *rampant, regardant,* within a circle of pellets resting his forepaws upon the arms of Spain.   Above, inscription giving the number of pieces to the kilogram (two pounds), and below the value.   *Rev., Hispania* seated upon a range of mountains, with an olive branch in her hand, surrounded by circle of pellets. Above, the number of GRAMOS (grains) weight, and below the date 1870.   Amadeus issued no copper coins during his brief reign.   Alfonso XII. succeeded in 1874, and in 1877-8-9 issued bronze pieces of five and ten Centimos.   *Obv.*—Head surrounded by ALFONSO XII POR LA GRACIA DE DIOS, date in exergue.   *Rev.*—Crowned arms on shield in wreath. Above REY CONST! DE ESPAÑA.   Value below CINCO or DIEZ CENTIMOS.

Of the Pretenders, "old" Don Carlos struck an 8 Maravedi piece with title of CARLOS V. in 1837, while during the "Carlist" war of 1875 were issued bronze 5 and 10 "Centimos

FIG. 20.—Five Centimos "de Peseta" of the Pretender Don Carlos, 1875.

de Peseta," imitating the coins of King Alfonso, with the laureated head and titles of CARLOS VII.

SPANISH PROVINCIAL ISSUES

Have all distinguishing features, which at once show the difference between them and national issues.

BARCELONA.—The capital of Catalonia has issued many copper coins, bearing her arms or name (BARCINO in Latin) or the busts and titles of her rulers. Philip III., IV. and V. of Spain, and Louis XIII. and XIV. of France are represented. The values are in "Ardites," "Seisinos," and "Dinerillos," and nearly all may be readily identified. The French occupying Barcelona from 1801 to 1814, struck pieces of $\frac{1}{2}$, 1, 2, and 4 quartos without date. *Obv.*—Arms, *Rev.*—Value. In 1823 were struck pieces of 3 and 6 quartos, with arms of Spain and titles of Ferdinand VII. on *obv.*, and the arms of the Province of Barcelona on the *rev.*

The BALEARIC ISLES (Majorca and Minorca) under Ferdinand VII. are represented by a piece of 12 "Dineros" of 1812. *Obv.*—Bust, *Rev.*—Arms.

BELLEPUIG by a "Seisino" of Louis XIII., 1642, with bust.

CATALONIA (Latin, CATHALUNA; Spanish, CATALUÑA) has an "Ardite" of Ferdinand VI., 1754–6, and a large coinage of different values bearing the arms and titles of Ferdinand VII., with 3 and 6 Cuartos of Isabella II., 1836–46.

GERONA (Latin, GERUNDA).—A "Seisino" of Louis XIII., 1642, with bust.

IVIÇA (Latin, EBUSIE).—"Dineros," with busts of Charles I. (*rev.* Arms), and Philip II. and III. (*rev.* Castle), 6 "Dineros" of Philip IV. and Charles II. (*rev.* Castle and value) and "Sueldo" of the latter; date 1668–86, with arms on *rev.*

MAJORCA (largest of the Balearic isles; Latin, MAJORICA). —"Doblers," with heads of Philip III., 1598–1621; Philip IV., 1621–65; and Charles II., 1665–1700, all with a cross on *rev.*; pieces of 1, 2, and 6 "Dineros" of Philip V.; *obv.* Head, *rev.* Cross; 6 "Dineros," 1724, Bust of Luis I. (Lud.), and 8 "Maravedis," 1823, with bust and arms of Ferdinand VII., and "P" for Palma (capital of Majorca).

NAVARRE.—This historic province has a long and interesting Numismatic record, illustrated by copper coins of its rulers. Up to the early part of the present century they are distinguished by combinations of figures and letters, and by the initials and monograms of rulers. The following is a concise list of such for identification: Philip II., "Dinero," 1608, *obv.* P.II.N.; *rev.* "P," between pillars of Hercules, "Cuarto," 1608–16, *obv.* PH. II, $\frac{FI}{4}$; *rev.* Arms and P-A., 2, 4, and 8 Maravedis, 1647, same general types. 4 Maravedis,

1650, "PHILIPPUS" in monogram.   Charles II., 2 Maravedis, 1655–1700, CAR.   Philip V., 2 Maravedis with PH.V. and $^{FI}_V$. Ferdinand VI., 1746–59, 2 and 4 Maravedis (square) with FERD VI and $^{FO}_{II}$.   Charles III., 1783–9, square 2 and 4 Maravedis with CAR VI.

From 1818 to 1826 were issued, in the various years, pieces of $\frac{1}{2}$, 1, 3, and 6 Maravedis of Ferdinand III. (VII. of Spain), which will be identified by the head and title above.   The $\frac{1}{2}$ Maravedi of 1832 is square, while 1 and 3 Maravedis of 1830–3 have the date on *rev.*

PAMPELUNA (in Navarre).—Ferdinand VII., 8 Maravedis, cast in gun-metal with P–8.   Isabella II., 1837, cast gun-metal. 8 Maravedis with 8-PP·M on *rev.*

VALENCIA.—Philip III., 1610–16 ; Philip IV., 1634–16, " Dinerillos," same type.   *Obv.*—Bust.   *Rev.*—Lily.

REPUBLIC OF ANDORRA.—This, the smallest independent territory in the world, possesses a piece of 10 Centimos inscribed, REPUBLICA DE LOS VALLS DE ANDORRA.   *Rev.* value and date 1873.

PORTUGAL.

The copper coinage of this portion of the Iberian peninsula commenced almost simultaneously with that of Spain, that is during the reign of the fifth ruler of the house of Aviz, Dom Emanuel, 1495 to 1521.   The Portuguese had not only the example of Spain as a precedent, but were accustomed to the native copper coins of their Indian possessions.   There is little chance of mistaking a Portuguese coin for one of any other series, for the arms are seldom absent.   They are composed of two shields, one within the other.   Arranged about the central shield are seven castles, while within it are five smaller shields arranged in the form of a cross.   In each of these, in turn, are five pellets ; above all, the royal crown.   Of Emanuel and John III., 1521–57, we have " Ceitils " with arms on *obv.*, and a three-towered castle rising from water, on *rev.*   Of the latter King there are also pieces of one and two " Reals " bearing JO III, besides other details.   The 10 " Real " pieces of John III. bear crowned arms on *obv.*, and on *rev.* a large " X." ''   On one he is styled REX QVINTVS DECIMVS, and on the other, REX SEXTVS DECIMVS.

Sebastian, 1557-78, is represented by a "Ceitil" with the three-towered castle, and the Real and its multiples, 3, 5, and 10, which may be identified by the name of the King, SEFASTIANVS, the phrase REX SETVS DECIMVS, or in the case of the 3 Real pieces which bear crowned arms, the characters L-3 or III-L being on the *rev.* There are no copper coins of "Cardinal" Henry who succeeded during two years. Dom Antonio, the Prior of Crato, an illegitimate grandson of Emanuel, attempted to sit upon the throne in 1580 in opposition to Philip II. of Spain, and having raised a small army, struck coins at Santarem. They are: a "Ceitil," *obv.* A, crowned, *rev.* a bird; a "Real," *obv.* Arms, *rev.* IN HOC SIGNO VINCES; 2 "Reals," *obv.* Arms, *rev.* a globe with IN . DEO; 4 "Reals," *obv.* Arms, *rev.* A (Angra). Philip II. of Spain became king of Portugal in 1580, under the title of Philip I., of whom there is a 10 "Real" piece upon which he is styled REX OCTAVVS DECIMVS. Philip II. and III. of Portugal do not seem to have had a copper coinage, and the first King of the present dynasty, the house of Braganza, John IV., ignoring the brief Spanish rule, styles himself REX XVIII on pieces of $1\frac{1}{2}$, 3, and 5 (v) Reis, 1640-56.

Of Peter II. there is a long and interesting series of several types. From this reign to the end there can be no mistakes made, as the dates and inscriptions are both clearly given. Peter II., 1667-1706, is represented by P II, crowned on a few

IG. 21.—One-and-a-half Reis of Peter II., 1700. (Type of others.

ot his coins, and John V., 1706-60, by J . V crowned. The values hereafter, are all expressed in Reis, sometimes by figures and sometimes by Roman numerals. Joseph I., 1750-77; Maria I. and Peter III. (conjointly), 1777-86; Maria I. (alone), 1786-1816, and the latter's son John, .as Prince Regent (P. REGENS) are represented by four or five

pieces each, of the common type. John, as Prince Regent,
1792–1816, and later as John VI., 1816–26, put· his bust on

FIG. 22.—Ten Reis of Maria I., 1799.   (Type of other rulers.)

thick brass pieces of 20 and 40 "Reis."   Peter IV., 1826–8,
issued a brass 40 "Reis" with bust.   Michael I., 1828–34,
and Maria II., 1828–53 (a period of Revolution, with rival
claimants), issued copper coins of the usual types.   Maria
struck in 1829–47 a thick piece of 40 "Reis," which is also

FIG. 23.—Forty Reis of John VI.   (Similar coin, as Prince Regent.

found counterstamped G. C. P. (Governo Civil, Porto). Louis I.,
1861–89, struck, first pieces of 3, 4, 10, and 20 "Reis" of the
old type, and latterly of 5, 10, and 20 "Reis" with his bust on
obv. surrounded by title. - The words VTILITATI PUBLICÆ will
frequently be found on the *rev.* of the earlier Portuguese copper
coins.   Portuguese colonial coins must not be confounded
with the home issues, to which they bear many points of re-
semblance.   Brazilian, African, and Indian issues exist, bearing

the names and titles of Portuguese monarchs back several hundred years. The type of their colonial issues, especially for Brazil, is that of a terrestrial globe with or without arms. References to Africa, Ethiopia, India, etc., in inscriptions, will indicate the difference. Coins for the Azores islands are inscribed PECVNIA INSULANA, or value in Arabic numerals of floral design ; for Madeira, PECUNIA MADEIRENSIS, for Terceira ILHA TERCEIRA, and for St. Thomas and Prince's Islands the coins are exactly like those of Brazil, with exception of the value on *rev.*, which is in Arabic numerals. These colonial issues are merely indicated to guard against errors, as they will at some future date be described in full.

GERMANY.

The copper coins of Germany, while not extending over a period of more than two centuries, present one of the most puzzling subjects with which one might well attempt to cope. Given first, the, up to recent times, division of that country into almost innumerable petty sovereignties, dukedoms and counties, which were independent of each other ; the existence of different expressions of value in each, the frequent changes of rulers, and the fact that but few of the coins bear other than the barest indications of their origin ; it becomes apparent that to be clear, the writer must go into a host of minute details, or be very brief. The dimensions of our present volume, however, leave no choice but the latter. Under these circumstances there is no possibility of observing other than the most convenient order in aiding to recognise, one by one, the different series. Where it would be necessary to quote different dates for every one of a long series of similar coins, dates inclusive of all are given.

PRUSSIA

Is at present the most important of the German States. Her copper coinage began with that of

BRANDENBURG under Frederick II., 1740–86, at a moment when *billon* had reached such a degree of baseness as to be practically worthless. The 1 and 3 Pfennings, and

$\frac{1}{2}$ Stuber will be known by "F.R." *script*, date, and value.
Frederick William II., 1786-97, is represented on $\frac{1}{4}$ Stuber
pieces and Schillings as "F.R.W." or "F.W." in *script*, value,
and date.   Also a Grossus, 1799, *Obv.* head, *Rev.* arms.
Frederick William III., 1797-1840, issued, first "Pfennings"
$\frac{1}{4}$ "Stubers" and a "Schilling" of preceding type, between
1810-16, 1 and 2 "Pfennings" having a sceptre in crowned
oval on *obv.*, while from 1821 to 1840 his copper coins
take the same type which they bear to the present day,
a spread eagle in a crowned shield, surrounded by inscription
denoting the number of like pieces amounting to a "Thaler"
on *Obv.*   Value, date, and SCHEIDE MUNZE on *Rev.*   The dates

FIG. 24.—Three Pfennings of Prussia, 1871.

subsequently are Frederick William IV., 1840-61, William I.,
1861-73, after which see German Empire.

POMERANIA.—Before the Prussian coinage begins, we
have copper coins of the Swedish occupation under Gustavus
III., 1776-92, 3 "Pfennigs" type, a Griffin, and K.S.P.L.M. ;
Gustavus Adolphus IV., 1806-1808, similar.   The town of
STRALSUND, a "Witten" and "Sechsling" of 1763, with

FIG. 25.—One Groschen of Dantzic, 1812.

three spear heads, and the town of WOLGAST, a "Witten"
of 1691-2, bearing Griffin.   DANTZIC (*Latin*, GEDANENSIS)
has a "Solidus" of 1766 with S.A. ; a "Schilling," 1801, with
F.W. ; and "Schilling" and Groschen of 1808-12, with arms

which are two small crosses, crowned in shield supported by Lions.

POSEN.—One and three "Groschen," 1816–17, with Eagle in oval shield.

SCHLESIEN.—Frederick William II., 1786–97, ½ Kreuzer F.W. *script.* "Solidus" and "Grossus" with F.W.R. on the latter in oval, and a "Grossus" with head on *Obv.*, arms on *Rev.* Frederick William III., 1797–1840, ½ "Kreuzer," 1806, *script.* F.W., 1 "Kreuzer," 1810. An eagle in crowned oval.

STOLLBERG.—Coppers of 1 and 1½ Pfennigs, through last century, bear a Stag.

FIG. 26.—One Pfennig of Stollberg, 1718–1801.

ERFURT.—1621–2, Values II, III, VI, XII, "Scherf," Arms, a wheel.

MULHAUSEN.—Pieces of II Pfennigs, 2 varieties, 1737 and 1767, with MVLHAVSER STADT MVNTZ.

QUEDLINBURG.—Coins from 1621 to 1662 bear in addition to Arms or other detail the letter "Q." Only the last two figures of date are usually given.

SCHLEUSINGEN has a "Heller" of Moritz William, 1705–26. *Obv.* "M.W." *Rev.* "SCHLEÜ'."

SAYN - WITTGENSTEIN. — "Pfenning " and quarter "Stuber" from 1752 have Arms in two oval shields.

MUNSTER. "Pfenning" and multiples 1661 to 1787 have *Obv.* St. Paul with Latin inscription, *Rev.* value in Roman numerals and date. 1 and 2 "Pfgs.," 1790, DOM CAPITUL.

Copper coins of the Bishops, *Obv. Script monogram, Rev.* value in Roman numerals. F(red'k) C(hristian) 1703. F(ranz) A(rnold), 1712–16; C(lement), 1735–55. Coins of the city, 1560–1758, bear STADT MUNSTER in addition to Arms and Roman numerals of value.

REINE.—Arms and STADT REINE, $\frac{1}{H}$(eller), III, IV, VI, VIII, XII "Pfgs.," etc.

PADERBORN (Bishopric). — Coins usually bear Arms with mitre, sword, and crozier, sometimes STADT PADERBORN

FIG. 27.—Four Pfennigs of Paderborn, 1743. (Clement August.

and Roman numerals of value. The Bishops from 1618 were Ferdinand I., to 1650; Theo(dore) Ado(lf), 1650–60; Fer dinand II., 1661–83; Her(man) Wer(ner), 1685–1703 ; Fran(cis) Arnold, 1706–18; Clement Aug(ustus), 1743–8; SEDE VACANTE (no Bishop existing), 1761; William Anton, 1766–7. Of the city there are "Pfennings" and multiples, of 1605–22 with STADT PADERBORN.

CORVEY.—1638, I and III "Pfgs." of Io(hn) CH(ristoph) ABB(ott) CORB. *Rev.* S. VITVS; I, III, IIII "Pfgs." of Arnold, 1640–48. *Obv.* Head of a steer. *Rev.* SANCTVS VITVS. Florence, 1696–1714; Maximilian, 1715–17, and a few successors are represented by similar coins.

Values of following coins run I, II, III, IIII, VI, and XII Pfennings.

ALEN.—Coins, 1584, bear STADT ALEN. Roman numerals.

BECKUM.—1595–1622, Coins bear STADT BECKUM. *Rev* Roman numerals.

BOCHOLT.—Coins, 1616–1762, bear Arms, a tree and STADT BOCHOLT. Roman numerals.

COESFELD.—1578–1663, Arms, head of steer, with STADT COESVELDT. Roman numerals.

DORTMUND.—1744–60, $\frac{1}{4}$ "Stuber." Arms, an eagle. Roman numerals.

DULMAN. — 1590–1625, Arms, a cross, with STADT DVLMAN. Roman numerals.

HALTERN.—1595–1624, Arms, a coiled cord, with STADT HALTEREN. Roman numerals.

HAMM.—1618–1746, Arms, three checkered lines, with STADT HAMM, etc. Roman numerals.

FIG. 28.—Three Pfennigs of Ham, 1717.

HERVORD.—1636–70, STADT HERVORD.

REITBERG (Province).—1654–1766, GRAFFSCHAFET REITBERG, or GR. RIDB. Coins of the city of Reitberg, 1617–51, STADT RITPE. Roman numerals.

RHEDA.—1655–9, Lion crowned. Roman numerals.

SOEST (*Latin* SUSATENSIS). — Arms, a key. Roman numerals.

TECHLENBURG-RHEDA.—1685, I, II, III, IIII "Pfennings." *Obv.* Arms and date. *Rev.* $_{\text{G.T.P.}}^{\text{I}}$, I, III, IV "Pfg." 1760–1, *Script monogram* "M(oritz) C(asimir)." Roman numerals.

WARBURG.—1622–3, I, III, III "Pfgs." Arms, two lilies, of which one inverted.

WARENDORF.—1574–1613, "Heller" and I, II, III, VI, XII "Pfg." Arms, a portcullis. 1690, I, II, III, III "Pfg.," St. Laurence standing, with S-L.

WIEDENBRUCK. — 1596–1619, Coins bear a wheel. Value in Roman numerals.

BERG.—M(ax) J(oseph), 1802–5, ½ "Stuber," *script monogram*. J(oachim) M(urat), 1806–7, III "Stubers" mon.

CLEVES.—Coins are "Dritts," 1670–1753 (varieties) DV or DVC CLIVIÆ. ¼ and 2 "Stubers," 1753–8, CLEVISCHE MUNTZ.

JULICH and BERG.—All coins bear inscription GULICH UND BERGISCHE. There are ¼ "Stuber" of 1750–51, Charles Theodore with arms, ¼ and ½ "Stuber;" 1765–94, same with "*C.F.*" *script* and 3 "Stuber," 1792–4, with Arms.

WIED.—1748 – 51, "Penning," *Obv. monogram. Rev.* SOLERTIA VINCIT. 1753, "Pfenning," *monogram, Rev.* value. 1750–52, ¼ "Stuber," BERG MUNTZ.

WIED-RUNKEL. — Always crowned *script monogram* "*G.W.*," 1 "Pfenning," 1751–52 ; 1 GVTER PFENNING, 1752 ; ¼ "Stuber," 1751–8.

COLOGNE (*German* CÖLN). — 1736 – 60, ¼ "Stuber," "*C.A.C.*" *script monogram.* 1764–7, "J.M.F." value and date. 1789, *Obv.* Double-headed eagle, BRODT PENNING. 1750–92, IIII HELLER. 1793, 8 HELLER : both with double-headed eagle bearing Arms.

TREVES (*German* TRIER).—1748–9, I, II, IIII "Pfgs.," "*F.G.C.*" *script.* 1757–64, I, II, III, IIII, VI "Pfgs.," and 1 "Kreuzer," "*J.P.C.*" *script monogram.* 1773, 1 "Heller."

FIG. 29.—Four Pfennigs of Treves, 1757.

Obv. Arms.   *Rev.* value and mint mark "*G.*" 1773–5, ¼, ½, and 1 "Kreuzer" of "CLEM(ent) WENZEL." *Obv.* Arms, 1789, I, II, III "Pfgs.," "*C.W.C.*" *script monogram.*

AIX LA CHAPELLE (*German* AACHEN).—Varieties of IIII "Pfg." and XII "Heller," 18th century, bear *Obv.* Eagle and date ; *Rev.* value and REICHS STADT ACHEN.

SCHONAU.—1755, *Obv.* double Eagle. *Rev.* HERRS-SCHÖNAW-IIII ("Hellers").

ELBERFELD.—Famine tokens, 1747. *Obv.* a Lion. *Rev.* Brod. 1/1 1817. *Rev.* BROD. 1/1

HOHENZOLLERN.—1842, 1 "Kreuzer," FURST HOHENZ-(ollern), etc., 1852. 1 Kr. *Obv.* An eagle, name in full.

BAVARIA.

(Arms—as below).

THE KINGDOM.—Copper coins all bear Arms. Series and values are I "Heller," 1761–1808; I and II "Pfgs.,"

FIG. 30.—Two Pfennigs of Bavaria (showing arms), 1871.

1761–1805; I "Heller," 1807–71; I "Pfg.," 1807–56; 2 "Pfg.," 1807–71; ½ "Kreuzer," 1851–56; I "Kreuzer," 1806.

CHUR-PFALZ.—1766, ZOLL-PFENNIG; 1773–95, ¼ and ½ "Kreuzer." *Obv.* Lion rampant in crowned oval, with C–P. *Obv.* value and dates.

PFALZ-ZWEIBRUCKEN.—1759–69, II and III "Kreuzers," CP crowned, value and P-Z. 1788, "Heller," ½ and I "Kreuzer." *Obv.* Lion and P-Z. *Rev.* Value and date.

BAIREUTH.—"Hellers," 1696–7, CE crowned. 1723–4, "G.W." *script.* 1730, "G.F.C." *script.* 1738–53, "F." *script.* 1767, "C.F." *script.* ½ and I "Kreuzer." 1752, *Obv.* "F." *script.* *Rev.* 28 and 14 STUCK MARCK.

FUGGER.—All 1622. I "Kreuzer" G. FF. L., 1–60 and 1–120 GULDEN. *Obv.* "*M.F.*" *in monogram* 1–160 GUL, "*M.Q.F.*" *in monogram.*

SPEYER.—1765, 2 "Pfg." and I "Kreuzer." *Obv.* Episcopal Arms and B-S. *Rev.* Value and date.

WURZBURG (Bishopric).—John Gottfried (Bishop), 1622, II and III "Pfg." and I "Krzr." Arms under "W." (*Rev.* of II "Pfgs." blank). Charles Philip Henry, 1751–53, ½ "Pfg.,' "C.P." *script,* I and 4 "Kr." LEICHTEN-KREUTZER. Adam Frederick, 1760–64, ½ "Pfg." 1760, "*Ʒ.A.F.*" *script monogram,* half "Kreuzer." *Obv.* Arms. *Rev.* "½ K.," no date; variety of same dated 17-62, ½ "Pfg." 1763–4, *Obv.* Arms. *Rev.* value. Ferdinand, 1810–11, I-VIERTEL (¼-)KRUZER and ½ KRUZER.

AUGSBURG.—Arms, a Fir-cone. 1608–22, *square* coins $\frac{1}{420}$ and $\frac{1}{210}$ "Gulden," values expressed CCCC-XX and CC-X.

FIG. 31.—Two Pfennigs of Augsburg.

1621–22, $\frac{1}{2}$ and 1 "Kreuzer," Arms. 1661–1708, *square* "Heller." 1740–72, *octagon* "Heller." 1760–1805, varieties of "Pfenning" and a II "Pfg." with Arms.

BAMBERG.—Arms, a Lion rampant behind oblique bar. 1662, I, II, III "Heller" and 1 "Kreuzer." *Obv.* Arms. 1761, I-GVTER HELLER. 1761–86, I-HELLER. 1761, a LEICHTER-PFENNING. 1762–3, $\frac{1}{2}$ LEICHTER KREVZER.

KEMPTEN.—(1622), 1–240, "Gulden." *Obv.* Eagle. *Rev.* CC-XXXX. 1 "Kreuzer," 1622, Eagle with "K" on breast.

LINDAU.—1663–94, Heller. *Obv.*—A tree. *Rev.* Blank.

NUREMBURG.—Arms, a half eagle and three bars. 1621, $\frac{1}{84}$ "Gulden." *Obv.* Arms. *Rev.* 84. 1622, 1 "Kreuzer," Arms with N above.

RATISBON (*German* REGENSBURG).—1677–1802, *octagon* "Heller." *Obv.* Crossed keys and R-H. *Rev.* Blank.

SCHWEINFURT, 1622.—Arms, an eagle, $\frac{1}{84}$ "Gulden." *Rev.* 84, 1 "Kreuzer." *Rev.* value.

WEISENBURG.—1622, 1 "Kreuzer." Eagle between towers of castle below W.

WURTEMBURG.

THE KINGDOM.—Arms, Three elk horns, later with

FIG. 32.—Half-Kreuzer of Wurtemburg (showing arms), 1864.

three lions. 1621-2, $\frac{1}{336}$ "Gulden." *Obv.* Arms and H. *Rev.* CCC-XXX-VI. 1622-3, "Heller" and "Kreuzer." *Obv.* Arms. 1687, "Krzr." *Obv.* Arms. *Rev.* VI-EINEN-KREITZER. 1840-71, $\frac{1}{4}$ and $\frac{1}{2}$ "Kreuzer." *Obv.* Arms. *Rev.* Value and date.

TEUTONIC ORDER.—1622, I, II, III "Kreuzers." *Obv* Cross and T.O. *Rev.* Value.

ISNY.—1695-6, "Heller." *Obv.* Eagle with horseshoe on breast. *Rev.* Blank.

RAVENSBERG.—Arms, Three chevrons. Coin I, II, III, VI, XII "Pfgs." bear Arms, and all or part of NVMIS RAVENS-BERG, dates and values.

RAVENSBERG (City).—Gateway of castle, "4" (Pfgs.) above, with or without date 1692-7. *Rev.* Blank.

ULM.—1621, *square* $\frac{1}{240}$ "Gulden." *Obv.* Arms. *Rev.* CC-XXXX, VI, "Heller," STADT MVNTZ undated. 1 Kreuzer, 1772-3, with Arms.

BADEN.

GRAND DUCHY.—Charles Frederick, 1746-1811, $\frac{1}{4}$, $\frac{1}{2}$, and 1 "Krzr." 1766, F.B.L.M., $\frac{1}{4}$, $\frac{1}{2}$, and 1 "Krzr." 1802, Arms. Charles, 1813-17, $\frac{1}{2}$ and 1 "Krzr.," G(ros) HERZOG-(thum) BADEN. Louis, 1818-30, $\frac{1}{2}$ and 1 "Krzr.," Arms $\frac{1}{2}$ and

FIG. 33.—One Kreuzer of Baden (showing arms), 1870.

1 "Krzr.," head. Leopold Charles, 1830-52, $\frac{1}{2}$ and 1 "Krzr.," Bust (large and small varieties) ; 1 "Krzr.," 1844, same. *Rev.* A statue. Frederick, 1852, $\frac{1}{2}$ and 1 "Krzr." ; 1856, Bust, 1 "Krzr." ; 1857-61. *Obv.* Bust. *Rev.* Inscription. 1859-71, $\frac{1}{2}$ and 1 "Krzr." ; Arms below BADEN. 1871, variety of latter with inscription on *rev*.

FURSTENBURG.—$\frac{1}{2}$ and 1 "Krzr.," 1772-3, Joseph Wenzel, Arms. 1 "Krzr.," 1804, Charles Joachim, Arms.

LOWENSTEIN-WERTHEIM.—1765–81, 1 and 2 "Pfgs.,"
Arms and L-W; 1 "Pfg." and 1 "Krzr.," *script monogram*
"*C.F.Z.L.*" 1790–1802, 1 "Pfg." with crowned C and F.L.W.S.M.
1791–1804, 1 "Pfg.," Arms, and L-W.

DUCHY OF BRUNSWICK AND LUNEBERG.

(LATER—KINGDOM OF HANOVER.)

DUKES.—Frederick Ulrich, 1620–21, I, II, and III "Pfennings," III "Flitter." *Obv.* Horse. 1621, I and III "Flitter."
Obv. Helmet. 1621–2, III and VI "Flitter." *Obv.* Leopards.
1621, I, II, and III "Flitter," and I, II, and III "Pfgs." *Obv.*
Lion.

LINE OF CELLE.—Christian, 1620–21, "Witten" and
"Sechsling." *Obv.* A Lion. I, II, and III "Pfgs.," GVD-PENN,
value above, date below. George William, 1687–9, 1 and 1½
"Pfgs." Horse and G.W. Varieties dated 1701–2–3, 1 and
1½ "Pfgs.," 1691–9, *monogram* "G.W."

ELECTORS OF BRUN' LUN' AND HANOVER.—
Ernest August, 1 and 1½ "Pfgs.," 1691–4, *script*, "*E.A.*"
George Ludwig (George I. of England), "Pfenning," 1699–
1709, *script*, G.L.C., 1718–22, 1½ "Pfg.," monogram of "*G.W.*"
Pfennings of 1717–23, "*G.R.*" *script*; 1725–6, St. Andrew and
cross; 1724–6, Wild man and tree. George Augustus (II. of

FIG. 34.—One Pfennig of Brunswick and Luneberg, 1730.

England), 1727–60, 1 and 1½ "Pfgs." with *script* "*G.R.*"
"Pfennings," 1729–39, St. Andrew and cross; 1730–60, Wild
man and tree. George III., also of England (king from 1814),
1760–1820, 1, 1½, II and 4 "Pfennings" various dates,
"*G.R.*" *script*, 1 and 4 "Pfgs." with St. Andrew, 1 "Pfg."
Wild man and tree.

KINGS.—George IV., 1820–30, 1, II and 4 "Pfgs.," "*G.R.*"
William IV., 1, II and 4 "Pfgs.," *script monogram* "*W.R.R.*,"

1 and 2 "Pfgs.," 1835–7.   HANNOVER SCHEIDE MUNZE.
Ernest August. 1838–51, 1 and 2 "Pfgs.," *monogram*, "*E.A.R.*,"

Fig. 35.—Two Pfennigs of Hanover (George V., Duke of Cumberland), 1853.

1839, variety ot 1 "Pfg." *Rev.* GLUCK AUF.   George V.,
varieties 1 and 2 "Pfgs.," crowned *script* "*G.R.*"

LINE OF WOLFENBUTTEL.—Anton Ulrich, 1704–14,
"Pfenning." *Obv.* Galloping Horse, ANT(on)ULR(ich) D.G.D(ux)
B(runswick) ET.L(uneberg).   *Rev.* I–PFENNING SCHEIDE MÜNTZ
(all Pfennings with Horse this type to end).   1708–13, 1½
"Pfgs.," Horse.   August William, 1714–31, "Pfennings."
Horse type and Wild man type.   Louis Rudolph, 1731–5,
"Pfennings."   "*L.R.*" *script*, and Horse type.   Ferdinand
Albert, 1735, "Pfenning," Horse.   Charles, 1735–80, 1, 1½
and II "Pfgs.," Horse; 1 "Pfg.," Wild man and tree.   1758,
a DENIER-HZ : BR : LU.–L.M. (latter an army token).   Chas.
William Ferdinand, 1780–1806, 1 and 2½ "Pfgs., Horse.
"Pfenning," Wild man.   Frederick William, 1813–15, "Pfen-
ning," Horse; II "Pfg.," *script*, "*FW.*"   Charles, 1816–30,
1 and II "Pfgs," Horse.   (These coins bear also titles of
Georges III. or IV. (of England) as guardians during minority,
till 1823.   Afterwards, Charles alone).   William, 1831–34,

Fig. 36.—Two Pfennigs of Brunswick, 1860.

1 and II "Pfgs.," Horse.   1851–6, 1 and 2 "Pfgs.," Horse,
without inscription.   1839–60, 1 and 2 "Pfgs.," Horse, surrounded by HERZOGTH BRAUNSCHWEIG.

VERDEN.—Arms, a cross in crowned shield.   1621, 1 "Schware," 1 "Grote," and "Double Schilling," *crowned monogram "S.P."*

SAXE-LAUENBURG, 1739-40.—$\frac{1}{2}$ "Dreiling" with *script* "*G.R.*" above small "s."   1839, same with Horse.

EAST FRIESLAND.—1753-1803, $\frac{1}{4}$ "Stubers."   *Obv.* *Script monogram "F.R."*   *Rev.* IIII-EINEN-STUBER (Fredk. II.). After 1763, *Rev.* $\frac{1}{4}$ STUBER (Fredk. William).   1823-5, $\frac{1}{4}$ "Stuber," *script "G.R."* over IV.

EIMBECK.—1620-21, 1 and III " Flitter " and 1 " Pfennig." Gothic " E "s, crowned.

GOTTINGEN.—Coins of seventeenth century bear name or a Gothic " G " crowned.

GOSLAR.—1620, 1 " Flitter," 1734-8, 1 "Pfg."   Both *Obv.* an eagle.   1737-64, *Obv.* the Madonna with MARIA MA·DOMINI. 1749-58, similar *Obv.*   *Rev.* 1 LEICHTER PFENNING.

HILDESHEIM.—1620, 1 "Flitter," Arms.   1662-70, 1 "Pfg.," *Obv.* Upper half of eagle.   Copper and brass grain token appeared 1626-58.   *Obv.* Arms. - *Rev.* ANNO 16(—).

OSNABRUCK.—Arms, a wheel.   During nearly two hundred and fifty years appeared at various dates pieces of from 1 to XII "Pfennings," with Arms and STADT OSNABRUCK (1570-1805).

OSTERODE.—1621, II "Flitter" with crowned "o." Variety, date only "-21."

SAXONY.

(DUCHIES, PRINCIPALITIES AND KINGDOM.)

SAXE-WEIMAR.—1750-5, 1 "Heller," 1, 1$\frac{1}{2}$ and II "Pfgs." "*F.J.D.S.*" *script* (Francis Josias with Ernest August Constantine as guardian).   1750-5, same coins, "*F.D.S.*" *script* (Frederick III., same guardian).   Ernest August Constantine (independently), "Heller," 1 and II "Pfennigs," 1756-8, "*E.A.C.*" *script*.   Anna Amelia, 1759-75, "Heller" and 1, 2 and 3 GUTER PFEN(nigs), crowned Arms.   Charles August, 1790-1813, "Heller," Arms.   1, 1$\frac{1}{2}$, 2, 3 and 4 "Pfennings" S.W.U.E.   1821-6, same coins with S.W.E.   Charles Frederick, 1830, 1, 1$\frac{1}{2}$, 2 and 3 "Pfgs." with S.W.E.   1840-51, 1 and 3

"Pfgs." with SACHSEN W.E. Charles Alexander, 1858–65,
1 and 2 "Pfgs." with SACHSEN W.E.

HENNEBERG.—1693-4, 1 "Heller." *Obv*. A hen.
Rev. ILME-NAUCH-HELLER.

FIG. 37.—One Heller of Henneburg, 1693.

GOTHA AND ALTENBURG.—Frederick II., 1692–1730,
"Heller." *Obv*. Arms. *Rev*. F.S.-GOTHA·U.-ALTENB-HELLER.
1712–27, "Heller," and 1718, "Pfennig," both with "*F.D.S.*"
script. 1729–32, 1½ "Pfg.," *script* "*F*," crowned. Frederick III.
1733–7, 1½ "Pfennigs,"*script* "*F*," crowned. 1744–50, "Heller,"
"Pfennig" and 1½ "Pfg." *Obv*. Arms. 1770, "Heller,"
"*G.U.A.*" *script*. 1752–61, 1½ and 3 "Pfg." *Obv*. Arms and
inscription. 1753–70, 1 and 1½ "Pfennigs," *script* "*F*" crowned.

SAXE-COBURG.—1680–99, 1 "Heller." *Obv*. "A" U.C.
crowned. *Rev*. CO-BURGER-HELLER.

SAXE-MEININGEN.—Anton Ulrich, 1755–61, 1 and 2
"Heller." *Obv*. Arms. *Rev*. 1 OR 2-MEINING-HELLER. 1761,
1 and 3 "Heller." *Obv*. "*A.V.*" *script monogram*. 1761–2,
1 "Heller." *Obv*. A hen. *Rev*. 1-MEININ :-HELLER. Charlotte
Amalia, 1768–9, two types "Heller." 1st, A hen ; 2nd,
Arms. *Revs*. like foregoing. Bernhard Erich Freund, 1803–
66. 1 "Heller," ¼, ½ and 1 "Kreuzer," 1 and 2 "Pfennings,"
all with Arms. 1839–42, 1 and 2 "Krzrs." with Arms between
"S—M." 1860–69, 1 and 2 "Pfennings" with SCHIEDEMÜNZE

SAXE-HILDBURGHAUSEN. — Ernest, 1703–14, "E
crowned and HILD-BURG H-HELLER. Ernest Frederick (I. and
II.), 1716–36, "Heller." *Obv*. *script* "*E.F.*" *Rev*. HH
HELLER. Ernest Frederick Charles, 1759–66, "Heller.
Obv. "*E.F.C.*" *script*. 1761–78, same *Obv*., Arms and usually
"H-H." 1759, "Pfennig" with Arms. 1763, 3 "Pfgs." with
Arms and inscription. Frederick, 1781–1806, "Heller."
Obv. Arms. *Rev*. H-H-HELLER. 1808–18, same with Arms
between S—H. 1809–23, ½ "Kreuzer," similar type. 1823–6,

"Pfg.," with Arms and inscription. 1820–25, 1, ¼ and ⅛ "Kreuzer," with *script* "*F.*"

SAXE-ALTENBERG.—1841–57, 1 and 2 "Pfennigs," with Arms and H. S. ALTENB(urg).

SAXE-SAALFELD.—John Ernest, 1688–1702, "Heller," SAAL-FELD-HELLER. 1719–24, *Obv.* "*J.E.*" *script*. *Rev.* Arms. 1730–63, "Heller," Arms (Chris. Ernest, to 1760). 1761–2, "Pfennig," "*F.J. D.S.*" *script* (Francis Joseph). Succeeding rulers, 1809–24, "Heller," Arms. 1809, Heller, *script* "*E.*" Various dates, 1770 to 1826, ½, 1, 1½, 3 and III "Pfennigs," Arms. 1809–20, 1, 2, 4 "Pfennigs," with *script* "*E.*" ("H.S.C.— S.S.M.")

SAXE-COBURG-GOTHA. — Various dates. 1834–56 (Ernst.) 1, 1½, 2 and 3 "Pfennigs." *Obv.* Arms.

THE KINGDOM OF SAXONY.—Frederick August III. Between 1772 and 1806 appeared 1 "Heller," 1 and III "Pfennigs." *Obv.* Arms of Saxony, with crossed swords. 1808 to 1825 (different dates), 1, 3, III and 4 "Pfennigs," with Arms only. Anton Clement, 1831–3, 1 and 2 "Pfennigs," with Arms. Successive Rulers, 1836–7, 1 and III "Pfennigs," Arms. 1841–61, 1 and 2 "Pfgs.," with Arms and "K.S.S.M." 1862–72, 1, 2, and 5 "Pfennings." *Obv.* Arms in oval with KOENIGREICH-SACHSEN. *Rev.* Value and date in circle, without SCHEIDEMÜNZE.

FIG. 38.—Five Pfennigs of Saxony, 1862

CAMENZ.—1622, 1 "Pfg." *Obv.* Wing of eagle, no date, 3 "Pfg." BONO-PUBL-CAM.

HESSE-CASSEL.

(Arms—A Lion).

Charles, 1723-4, "Heller." *Obv.* Lion. 1727-30, "Heller." 1727, II "Heller." Both having *monogram* "CL." 1726-8, III "Heller" with bust. Fred. I. bet. 1730-50, I and I½ "Hellers" *script. mon.* "*F.R.*" 1730-43, "Heller" with *monogram* FR. 1733-51, II "Heller," monogram "F.F." 1733, III "Heller," "HF." 1735-48, III "Heller," Bust and REX.-SUECIAE. William VIII. 1751-8, I and II "Heller," w between Z—H, L above. 1758-9, *script monogram* "*W.L.L.*," 1755, III "Heller," Bust and HASS-LANDG(raf). Fredk. II., 1760-85, I, III, IIII, 2, 3, 4, 6 and 8 "Heller," with double "*FL*" *script monogram*. 1774-5, I "Heller," Lion. 2, 4 and 8 "Heller," Lion with shield, and *script* "*F.L.*" 1783, ¼, ½ and I "Kreuzer," Arms and HESSE-CASSEL. William IX., 1788-94, 2 and 4 "Heller," *script* "*W.L.*" 1791-1803, I and 3 "Heller," *script monogram*, "*IV*" and "*LL.*" 1790, I "Heller," Lion. 1801-3, ¼ and ½ "Kreuzer," Arms HESSE CASSEL. 1803-4, ½ "Kr.," Arms and KUR HESSEN. 1803-21, I, 2 and 4 "Heller," *script monogram* "*W.K.*" William, 1822-31, I, 2 and 4 "Heller," similar to last. 1824-35, ¼, ½ and I "Kreuzer," Arms and KUR-HESSEN. William and Fredk. Wm. (1847), 1843-66, I, 2 and 3 "Heller." *Obv.* Arms and 360, 180, or 120 EINEN THALER. *Rev.* KURHESSISCHE SCHEIDEMUNZE, value and date. 1859-72, I "Pfg." Arms and inscription.

HANAU-MUNZENBURG.—William VIII., 1739-46, I and II "Heller," *script* "*W* and *LL.*" 1752-7, I "Heller." *Obv.* Z$_W^L$H. *Rev.* Value, SCHEIDE-MUNTZ. William IX., 1768-73, "Heller," Arms and W.E.P-Z-H. 1773, "Kreuzer," Arms and HESS HANAU MUNTZENB.

SCHAUMBURG.—Arms, a Nettle-leaf. Ernest, 1620, I½, III and VI "Pfgs," Arms and ERNST. 1769-85, "Pfennig," Arms "F.L." *Rev.* GUTER PFENNIG. 1787-1803, same, Arms, "W.L." 1804-32 same, Arms, "*WK*."

SCHMALKALDER.—1720-8, "Heller" and I½ "Pfg." *Obv. script* "C.L." *Rev.* Value and ins. 1730-44, "Pfenning" and "Heller," *script* "*F.R.*" 1730, I "Pfg." *mon.* "*F.R.*" 1754, same, *script* "*W.L.*"

FULDA, 1759, II "Heller," *Obv. script* "*A.F.E.*" *Rev.* F.F.L.M. 1769, Pfennig, *Obv.* H.E.F. *Rev.* same as before.

WESTPHALIA.

(Arms—similar to those of Bruns.' Lun.').

Ferdinand, 1619–20, III, VI and XII "Pfg." MO. DVC. WESTPH. undated, also XII "Pfg," dated.   Jerome Napoleon (Bonaparte) 1807–15, I and II "Pfgs," 1, 2, 3 and 5 centimes, with mono-

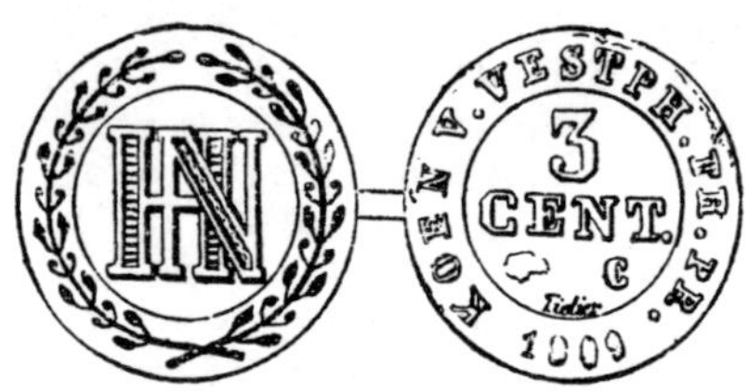

FIG. 39.—Three Centimes of Westphalia (Jerome Napoleon Bonaparte), 1809.

gram HN. *Rev.* KOEN. V. WESTPH. FR. PR, and date, sunk on raised rim; value, date and mint mark in field.

HESSE-DARMSTADT.—Ernest Louis, 1735, I, II, III, IIII and VI "Pfgs." *Obv. script* "*E.L.*" *Rev.* ANNO DOMINI and date.   Louis IX., 1773–90, coins bear on *Obv.* a lion, and H-D.   Varieties of "I Pfennig" and "II Pfennigs."   Succeeding rulers, 1791–7, "Pfg." Lion and HESSEN-DARMST. 1798–1806 "Pfennig," Lion and H-D. 1805 (Louis X.), ½ "Stuber" with *script* double "*L*" and X.   1811–16, varieties ¼ and ½ "Kreuzer" with Arms and G.H.—E.M., etc., or G(rosherzogthum) HESS," etc.   1824–55 "Heller," Arms and "G.H—K.M."

MAYENCE (*German* MAINZ).—Arms, a wheel.   John Fredk. Charles, 1759–61, 1, 2 and 3 "Pfgs.," with "*J.F.C.*," *script mon.*, surmounted by coronet, a small wheel below. 1756–61, 1 "Heller," 1, II, 2 and 3 "Pfgs." with Arms. in elaborate cartouche, surrounded by long inscription commencing I.F.C.D.G., etc.   1760, 2 and 3 "Pfgs." *Obv.* Bust and titles.   Emerich Jos., 1766, I, II and III "Pfgs." with Arms. 1768–71, I, II and III "Pfgs." Arms and inscription. 1769–70, "Heller" and "Pfennig," with Arms and E-J., and "Heller" with *script mon.*, "*E.J.*"   Fredk. Chas. Jos., 1779–81, "Pfennig" with Arms, and "Pfennig" with F.C.J.K. 1795, ¼ and ½ "Kreuzer."   *Obv.* Bust and titles.   *Rev.* Value, date and KVR.

MAINZER LAND MVNTZ. Charles Theod., 1808–12, 1 "Heller" (SCHEIDE MÜNZ), Arms and ins.

SIEGE PIECES.—In 1793 the French besieging Mayence struck pieces of 1, 2 and 5 "sols," with *Obv.* Fasces and lib.

FIG. 40.—Two Sols, struck by the French forces besieging Mayence, 1793.

cap surrounded by REPUBLIQUE FRANCAISE, 1793 L'AN 2ᴱ. *Rev.* MONOYE DE SIEGE DE MAYENCE around value.

GRAND DUCHY OF MECKLENBURG.

(Arms—The Face of an Ox).

MECKLENBURG-SCHWAREN.—Adolf Fred'k., 1621–2, 1, II and III "Pfennigs," with Arms. Fredk. Wm., 1704, 1½ Pfennigs, *mon.* "F.W." Chris. Ludwig., 1752–9, 1, 3, III and 6 "Pfennigs," with Arms. 1759, III and 6 Pfennigs with *script* "F," crowned. Fredk. Francis I., 1831, 1 and 2 "Pfennigs," *script*, "F.F." Fredk. Francis II., 1843–64, 3 "Pfgs," with *script* "F.F." 1872, 1, 2 and 3 Pfgs, *script* "FF," with inscription.

MECKLENBURG-GUSTROW.— Hans Albrecht, 1621–2, 1, II and III "Pfennigs," Arms. Gustavus Adolphus, 1674–92, III "Pfennigs." *Obv.* Monogram "GA." *Rev.* LAND WITT.

MECKLENBURG-STRELITZ.—Adolph Fredk. III., 1747, III "Pfennigs," Arms. 1752, 1 "Pfg." *script* "A.F." Adolph Fredk. IV., 1753–5, III "Pfennigs." Arms, 1760. 3 GVTE PFENNING, *script* "A.F." 1764–94, same, "Æ." George, 1838, 1 and 1½ "Pfennig." 1832–59, III "Pfennigs." All with Gothic **G** crowned. Fredk. Wm., 1862–24, III "Pfg," with *script* "F.W." 1872, 1, 2 and 5 "Pfennig" with same and inscription.

ROSTOCK.—Arms, a Griffin, on all coins. 1747–1858, a "Pfennig." 1710–64, III "Pfg." 1761, 2 "Pfgs." 1815–64, 3 "Pfgs."

WISMAR.—Arms, head of an Ox (profile). 1662, II "Pfg." Arms. 1621–1845, III "Pfg." Arms. 1762, 6 "Pfg." Arms. 1854, 3 "Pfgs.," Arms under helmet. (Square necessity pieces in gun metal were struck in 1715 to values of 4, 8, 16 and 32 "Schellings," 4 and 8 "Marks." M.N.W., on these coins represents "Moneta Nova Wismariensis").

DUCHY OF NASSAU.

(GERMAN—HERZOGTHUM NASSAU.)

(Arms—A Lion Rampant.)

WEILBURG LINE.—Charles August, 1752, II and III "Kreuzer," *script* "*C.A.*," between "F.-N." Fredk. Wm., 1808–14, ¼, ½ and varieties of 1 "Kreuzer," with Arms and inscription. William, 1817–22, ¼ and 1 "Kreuzer" with Arms, etc. 1830–8, 1 "Kr." with *Rev.* EIN KREUZER. Adolph, 1842–56, 1 "Heller" and 1 "Kreuzer," with Arms. 1859–63, 1 "Pfg." and 1 "Kr.," Arms supported by Lions.

ORANGE LINE.—1766–91, I and II "Heller," *script monogram* "*O.N.N.*"

OLDENBURG.

(Arms—Two bars *l.*, cross *r.*)

PROVINCE.—1802–16, ½ "Grote." *Obv.* Arms. *Rev.* Value and O.L.M. Paul Fredk. Augt., 1831–46, varieties ½ "Grote" like preceding. 1846–52, ¼ "Grote" and 1 "Schwaren," with *script* "*P.F.A.*" Nicholas Fredk. Peter, 1853–69, ½ "Grote," 1 and 3 "Schwaren," all with *script* *N.F.P.* etc.

OLDENBURG-BIRKENFELD. — Paul Fredk. August, 1848, 1, 2 and 3 "Pfg.," *script* initials, etc. Nicholas Fredk. Peter, 1858–59, 1, 2 and 3 "Pfg.," *script* initials, etc.

JEVER.—Fredk. Aug., 1764, "Heller" and "Pfennig." *Obv.* Bust. *Rev.* Arms. Paul I. (of Russia), 1799, ¼ "Stuber." *Obv.* Lion in crowned shield.

ANHALT.

(Arms —A Bear walking on wall).

Fig. 41.—Coin of Anhalt Bernberg.

ANHALT-BERNBERG.—1746–95, Victor Fredk. to Fredk. Albert, 1, 1½ and 2 "Pfennings," with Arms. Various details. Alex. Fredk. Christian, 1797–9, 1 "Pfg.," Arms. 1807–31, 1 and 4 "Pfennigs," *script* "*A.F.C.*" Alex. Charles, 1839–40, 1 and 3 "Pfennigs" (280, and 96 EINEN THALER, respectively). 1856–62, 1 and 3 "Pfg." (360 and 120 EINEN THALER, resp.). All with arms.

ANHALT-DESSAU.—Leopold, 1836–7, 1 and 3 "Pfg.," similar to foregoing.

ANHALT-ZERBST.—1760, 1 "Heller" and 1 "Pfennig." Bust, Arms and F.A.Z.L.M.

LIPPE.

(Arms—A heraldic Rose.)

1621, III "Flitter," Arms. Undated, but early, ½, 1, 1½, II, III and VI "Pfennig." Arms and LIPP. LAND MUNTZ. 1763,

Fig. 42.—One Pfennig of Lippe, 1802.

½, 1 and II "Pfg.," *script mon.* "*S.A.*" 1760, 1 "Heller," Arms. 1763–1840, varieties, II "Heller," 1, 1½ and II "Pfg.,"

Arms, etc. 1847–58, 1 and 3 "Pfennig," crowned Arms, 12 and 4 EINEN SILBER GROSCHEN," resp.

SCHAUMBURG-LIPPE.—1750, William Ernst, 1 "Pfennig," Arms. 1824–6, George William, 1 GVTER PFENNIG. *Obv.* Rose and nettle-leaf. 1858, 1, 2, 3 and 4 "Pfennig," with crowned *script mon* "G.W." *Rev.* Parts of a Thaler.

SCHWARZBURG-SONDERHAUSEN.—1846–58, 1 and 3 "Pfennigs." 1852–66, ¼ and 1 "Kreuzer," all Arms.

SCHWARZBURG-RUDOLSTADT. — 1751–62, John Fredk., 1, II and 3 "Pfg.," *script* "*J.F.*" *Rev.* Inscription. 1769–1783, Ludwig Gunther IV., "Heller," ½ and 1 "Pfennig," with *script* "*L.G.*" 1792, Charles Fredk., ½ and 1 "Pfg.," *script,* "*C.F.*" 1801–4, Ludwig Fredk., 1 and 3 "Pfg.," SCHWARZ-RVD-L.M., etc. 1812–25, Fredk. Gunther, 1, 2, 3 and 4 "Pfg.," *script* "*F.G.*" 1840–56, ⅛, ¼, ½ and 1 "Kreuzer," Arms. 1842, 1, 2 and 3 "Pfennig," FÜRSTENTH. SCHWARZBURG, R. 1857–72, ¼ and 1 "Kreuzer," SCHEIDE MÜNZ.

WALDECK.

(Arms—A Star of eight points.)

1622, Christian and Walrath IV., I, III, IIII and VI "Pfg." *Obv.* WALDECK. *Rev.* LANT-MUNTZ. 1638, Wal. IV., Philip and Johann ; 1 and II "Pfg." *Obv.* WOLR. PHIL. IOHAN. *Rev.* WALDE LANTMV. 1693, Christian Ludwig, I, II, III, IIII and VI. Arms (star and cross) in oval. 1730–61, Charles Aug., I, II, III, IIII and VI "Pfgs.," crossed "C."s 1773–1810, Fredk., 1 and III "Pfg.", *script* "*F.*" 1779–1810, 1 and

FIG. 43.—Three Pfennigs of Waldeck, 1781.

III "Pfg." and ½ "Groschen." Arms and ins. 1816–17, Geo. Henry, 1 "Pfg.," *script* "*G.H.*" 1816–25, 1 "Pfg." Arms and inscription. 1819–25, 1, 3 and III "Pfg." Arms. 1821–

25, 1 "Pfg." and ½ "M.(arien) Groschen."   Arms of Waldeck and Pyrmont (Star and cross).   1842–5, 1 and 3 "Pfgs." Arms (Wal. + Pyr.).   360 and 120 EINEN THALER, resp.   1855– 67, George Victor, 1 and 3 "Pfgs.," similar.

PYRMONT (separately) 1761, I, II and IV "Pfgs."   Crowned cross.

REUSS.

UPPER GREITZ.—1760–89, Henry XI., 1 "Heller," ½, 1 and II "Pfennigs." *Obv.* Arms (a Lion). *Rev.* G. (or F-) R. P.-GREIZER-L.M.   1760–1, 1 and II "Pfg.," REVSS-SCHEIDE- MVNZE.   1800–33, successive rulers, 1 "Heller," 1 and 3 "Pfg." Lion type as above.

REUSS-GERA.—1761, Henry XXX., 1 and 2 "Pfg." *Obv.* Head of dog. *Rev.* G.R.P.-GERAISCHE-L.M.

REUSS-SCHLEITZ.—1815–16, Henry XLII., 3 "Pfg." *Obv.* Lion. *Rev.* F.R.P.-SCHLEIZER-L.M.   1841–7, Henry LXII., 1 and 3 "Pfgs.," FURSTENTHURM REUSS-SCHLEIZ, etc.

REUSS-LOBENSTEIN.—1812, Henry LI., 1, 2, 3 and 4 "Pfg." *Obv.* Head of dog. *Rev.* F.R.P. EBERSDORF. L.M. 1841, Henry LXXII., ½ "Pfg.," Lion without ins.   1841–4, 1 and

FIG. 44.—One Pfennig of Reuss, 1864.

3 "Pfgs.," Arms, FURSTENTH. REUSS. LOBENST. EBERSD.   1850 –68, same, with IUNGERER LINE added to ins.

FRANKFORT (on the Maine).
(Arms—An Eagle.)

1767–1863, "Hellers" and I and II "Pfennigs," with Arms, etc. Various dates. *ins.* " F(rei) STADT FRANKFÜRT."

BREMEN (Hanse Town.)
(Arms—A Key.)

1719–1852, 1 "Schwaren," Arms, etc.   1797–1866, 2½ "Schwaren," *do.*   1841, ½ "Groten," *do.*

GERMAN EMPIRE.

1873, 1 and 2 " Pfgs." (copper), 5, 10 and 20 " Pfgs." (nickel),
Obv. Imperial Eagle.   *Rev.* DEUTSCHES REICH and date.

FIG. 45.—Two Pfennings of the German Empire, 1874.

value, large figure in field.   The Emperor William II. has just
slightly modified this series, substituting a new and very handsome Imperial Eagle, which quite fills the *Obverse*, for the
previous smaller one.

SCANDINAVIA.

The bold Norsemen have employed copper as a medium of
exchange from a very remote antiquity, but did not coin it
into the convenient shape to which we are accustomed until
the rest of Europe had begun to do so.   Even then, it was
some years before the old system ceased to hold its place by
the side of the new.

The old Norse copper coinage reminds strikingly of the
early money of Rome as elsewhere alluded to, being composed
of precisely similar blocks or slabs of pure copper, often many
pounds in weight.   These were first roughly stamped with an
indication of weight or value in " Dalers," but later were marked
by being punched hap-hazard from five to a dozen times with
the impression of such circular dies as were used for striking
small round coins.   *Klippe*, or square coins, were also common
at one time, a flat bar of copper being struck with one square
impression after another on both sides, and then chopped into
the squares thus indicated.

DENMARK.

(Arms—Three lions on field interspersed with small hearts.)

The substitution of copper for billon in small values occurred about the time of the reign of

CHRISTIAN IV., 1588–1648, who issued a " Pfennig," with crowned " C " and date 1602, and in 1624 a " Sosling," with his bust and titles.

FREDERICK III., 1648–70, is represented by "Soslings " of 1651. Types, crowned " F3," or Arms on *Obv.*

CHRISTIAN V., 1670–99, issued square pieces (*Klippe*) of 2, 4 and 8 " Skilling " value, with his cipher, " C5 " on *Obv.* They were probably siege pieces, struck at Christiania, Sweden. Also a very pretty little half " Skilling," *Obv.* his bust and CHRIST. V. DEI GRATIA. *Rev.* A crown surrounded by DAN, NOR, GOT, VAN, REX, and date.

FREDERICK IV. issued pieces of 1 and ½ SKILLING DANSKE,

FIG. 46.—Half Skilling of Frederick IV., 1699.

dated 1719. The *Obv.* containing a curious crowned *script monogram* of " 4*FF*4," with wreath.

CHRISTIAN VI.—1730–46, A " Skilling " bears crowned *mon.* " *C6.*"

FREDERICK V.—1746–56, A ½ " Skilling " has *crowned mon.* F5.

CHRISTIAN VII.—1766–1808, ½ and 1 " Skilling " bear crowned monograms, the ½ " C7," the 1 " 7CC7," date 1771.

FIG. 47.—Half Skilling of Christian VII.

FREDERICK VI.—1808–39. Pieces of 1, 2, 3, 6 and 12 "Skilling." *Obv.* Bust. *Rev.* Arms and date. 1809–12 struck for Iceland, also "Skilling," 1812, crowned "FVI" for Iceland. From 1813 to 1818 were struck a large series of 1, 2, 3, 4, 6—12, and 16 "Skillings," with *Obv.* Arms. *Rev.* RIGSBANKTEGN (State Bank Token). Value and date. In 1818, ½ and "1 RB. SK." of this series exist. A ½ "RB. SK." of 1838 has—*Obv.* "FVI." crowned.

CHRISTIAN VIII.—1839–48, Represented by series of ⅕, ½, 1 and 2 R.B.S. (Rigsbank Skillings). *Obv.* Head, name and titles. *Rev.* Crowned sword and sceptre, value and date.

FREDERICK VII.—1848–67, ½ "Skilling" (R.B.), with crowned "FVII," and "Skilling." *Obv.* Head. *Rev.* Crowned

FIG. 48.—One Skilling of Frederick VII.

sword and sceptre, etc., (large or small head), dates. 1852, ½ and 1 "Skilling," (brass), RIGSMONT "FVII," crowned between 1856–63.

CHRISTIAN IX.—1867– , ½ and 1 "Sk.," RIGSMONT, 1852

FIG. 49.—Five Öre of Christian IX., 1874.

(brass), "CIX," crowned. 1, 2, and 5 Ore, 1874. *Obv.* Crowned "CIX" and date. *Rev.* Value, dolphin, and spear of wheat.

SCHLESWIG-HOLSTEIN.

CHARLES FREDERICK, 1706.—$\frac{1}{12}$ "Schilling." *Obv.* Crowned "C.F." *Rev.* 12-EINEN-SCHILLING.

CHRISTIAN VII., 1787.—"Dreiling" ($\frac{1}{3}$), and "Sechsling" ($\frac{1}{6}$). *Obv.* Crowned *script mon.* "C.R." *Rev.* Value, etc.

NORWAY.

(Arms—A Lion treading on or wielding curved battle-axe.)

As this state was associated with Denmark until 1814, when it was joined to Sweden, its coinage up to the reign of Frederick VI. is in most respects identical. However, pieces struck in or for Norway are usually distinguished by two tiny hammers, crossed, as a mint mark. 1, 2, and 4 "Skillings," COURANT, with a crowned *mon.* "F.R." on *Obverse* were the last copper coins of the last Danish king of Norway—Frederick VI. The Swedish line begins with—

CHARLES XIII., of whom there is a "Skilling." *Obv.* Arms dividing C^{L}—XIII. *Rev.* 1-SKILLING SPECIES-1816.

CHARLES XIV., JOHN (The French General Bernadotte) 1818–44.—$\frac{1}{2}$, 1, and 2 "Skilling" SPECIES. Same type as the former. Norwegian Arms dividing C$^{\text{L}}_{\text{XIV}}$—JOH.

CHARLES XV., 1859–72.—1 and varieties $\frac{1}{2}$ "Skilling." Arms dividing, C^{L}—XV.

FIG. 50.—One Skilling of Charles XV.

OSCAR II, 1872- .—1, 2, and 5 "Ore." Type—Arms dividing O^{CR}—II. *Rev.* Value in wreath, date.

SWEDEN.

(Arms—Three Crowns.)

Besides the huge masses of copper hitherto alluded to, Sweden did not make use of that metal to express minor values till along in the 16th century. Her round copper coins of convenient size did not appear until about the time of Gustavus Vasa, and are not common until the reign of

JOHN III., 1570–92, pieces of whose coinage bear the Arms on both faces.

SIGISMUND, 1597–9, has left a half "Ore" with his initials "S-R" (Sigismund Rex) and Arms under.

GUSTAVUS II., ADOLPHUS. Copper coins became very plentiful, both in *Klippe* form and round. Of the square pieces the values are 1 "Fyrk," ½, 1 and 2 "Ore." Various

FIG. 51.—*Klippe* or Square Öre of Gustavus Adolphus.

types—usually the three crowns interspersed with "G-A-R" and date. *Rev.* Crowned Arrows (crossed) or *Fasces* and value. The *round* pieces—1 "Fyrk," ½ or 1 "Ore"—have on *Obv.* Arms or *Fasces. Rev.* Crowned Arrows, Griffin, or Eagle. These early round coins appear to be cast, though finely done, and the "Ore" is from 1½ to 2 inches in diameter. The workmanship elaborate and inscriptions very long. The full inscription on a coin of Gustavus Adolphus would be— *Obv.* "GVSTAVUS ADOLPH D. G. SVEG(orum) GOTH(orum) VAN (dalorum) REX. M. PR. *Rev.* MONETA NOVA CVPREA "NICOP-ING" ("DALARENSIS" or "ARBOGENSIS") MDCXXVIII (or other date), the last word preceding being the name of city where struck, "G-A-R" or "G-A-R-S," alway appears somewhere on his coins.

CHRISTINA.—1632–55. Several fine large coins of previous type with "C-R-S."

FIG. 52.—Öre of Christina (cast), 1650.

CHARLES X., GUSTAVUS—1654–60. $\frac{1}{6}$ "Ore." *Obv.* Arms with "C-G-R-S." *Rev.* Crowned Lion.

CHARLES XI.—1660–97. Large "Ores," fractions and multiples thereof, of usual types with "C-R-S." The mint

FIG. 53.—One-sixth Öre of Charles XI.

marks "K.M." and "S.M." mean "Koppar Mynt" and "Silfver Mynt."

CHARLES XII.—1697–1718. Pieces of $\frac{1}{6}$ "Ore." *Obv.* Lion, crowned or in shield. *Rev.* Three crowns "CXII R.S." and date. During the wars of Charles his prime minister, one Baron von Goertz, replenished the depleted Treasury by a series of "Dalers" in Copper, bearing nearly all on *Obv.* a mythological figure with name above and date below. On *Rev.* of all "I-DALER-S.M." in cartouche. The series in full is :

1715.—1. A Crown.   2. "Publica Fides."   1717.—3. "Wett och Wapen."   1718.—4. "Flink och Fardig."   5. Jupiter.

FIG. 54.—"Necessity" Daler of Baron Goertz, Prime Minister of Sweden.

6. Phœbus.   7. Saturnus.   8. Mars.   9. Mercurius.   1719.—10. Hoppet.   11. Bust, "GEORG HEINR BARO DE GOERTZ." *Rev.* NESCESSITAS CARET LEGE-I-DALER-S.M.   There is also a little piece of poor workmanship bearing *Obv.* a laureated head, the eye being noticeable by its blind expression.   *Rev.* A little figure of Mercury.   This may be a half or even quarter "Daler."   The substitution of his own head for that of his Queen (first year of Ulrica Eleanora) cost him the original model of his spirited portraiture.

ULRICA ELEANORA.—1719–20.   1 "Ore."   *Obv.* Crowned shield with arrows.   *Rev.* Three crowns and "V.E.R.S."   Many of these pieces are struck over "Goertz Dalers," as are the "Ores" of her successor.

FREDERICK I.—1720-51.   ½ and 1 "Ore" of preceding

FIG. 55.—Reverse of One Öre of Frederick I.   Showing Arrow *type* common to series

type (1720–50), 1 "Ore" with crowned *script mon.* "*F.F.*," and 2 "Ore" with "F.I.S.G.V.R."

ADOLF FREDERICK.—1751–71.   Size of "Ore" increased. "Ore" has crowned monogram "Æ."   *Rev.* Crowned arrows,

value and date.   1 "Ore," 1768, has "A.F.R.S.," and 2 "Ore"
"A.F.S.G.V.R."

Fig. 56.—Two Öre (silfver mynt) of Adolf Frederick, 1766.   *Rev.* Arrows.

GUSTAVUS III.—1771–92.   "Ores."   Types "G-R-S" and
"G.III" crowned.   2 "Ore," 1777, "GIII S.G.V.R."
GUSTAVUS IV., ADOLF.—1792–1809. $\frac{1}{4}$ and $\frac{1}{2}$ "Skilling."

Fig. 57.—One-fourth Skilling of Gustavus IV. Adolphus.

Three Crowns on Globe. $\frac{1}{12}$, $\frac{1}{4}$, $\frac{1}{2}$ and 1 "Skilling," crowned
"GA IV."   *Rev.* Arrows, value and date.
CHARLES XIII.—1809–18. $\frac{1}{12}$ "Skilling" (1812).   "CXIII"
crowned.   *Ins.* FOLKETS VAL MIN HOGSTA LAG.   *Rev.* 3

Fig. 58.—One-twelfth Skilling of Charles XIII.

Crowns, value and date. $\frac{1}{4}$, $\frac{1}{2}$ and 1 "Skilling," crowned
mon. "C.C."

CHARLES XIV., JOHN.—1818–44. 1st series : $\frac{1}{12}$, $\frac{1}{6}$, $\frac{1}{4}$, $\frac{1}{2}$ and 1 "Skilling." Previous type. *Obv.* Crowned "CXIV." *Ins.* FOLKETS KÄRLEK MIN BELÖNGING. *Rev.* Arrows, value and date. 2nd series, 1832–3 : $\frac{1}{6}$, $\frac{1}{4}$, $\frac{1}{2}$ and 1 "Skilling." *Obv.* Bust and titles. *Rev.* 3 Crowns, value and date. 3rd series, 1835–44 : $\frac{1}{6}$ and $\frac{1}{4}$ "Skilling." "CXIV" crowned. 4th series, 1835–43 : $\frac{2}{3}$, 1 and 2 "Skilling," "BANCO." *Obv.* Bust as before. *Rev.* Value, Arrows and date in wreath.

OSCAR I.—1844–59. 1st series, 1844–55 : $\frac{1}{6}$ and $\frac{1}{3}$ "Skilling." *Obv.* Crowned "O." *Ins.* RATT OCH SANNING. *Rev.* "BANCO" type. 2nd series : $\frac{2}{3}$, 1, 2 and 4 "Skilling." *Obv.* Young Bust and titles. *Rev.* as before. $\frac{1}{2}$ "Ore," 1856–8. Crowned "O" as before. 3rd series, 1856–8 : 1, 2 and 5 "Ore." *Obv.* Head and titles. *Rev.* Value and date within wreath.

CHARLES XV.—1859–72. 1st : $\frac{1}{2}$ "Ore," 1867. "C.C."

FIG. 59.—Five Öre of Charles XV., 1857.

crowned. 2nd : 1, 2 and 5 "Ore" of previous type (Bust, etc.).

OSCAR II.—1872– . 1, 2 and 5 "Ore," 1873. Busts, etc., as before. 2nd series, 1874– : 1, 2 and 5 "Ore." *Obv.* "OII" crowned. *Ins.* BRODRAFOLKENS VAL. *Rev.* Value, date and three Crowns in circle.

AUSTRIA.

(Up to 1806 joined with Germany and northern Italy as
the " Holy Roman Empire.")

(Arms—A double-headed Eagle—*German name*, OESTERREICH.)

MARIA THERESA.—The copper coinage of Austria proper
appears to begin in the reign of Maria Theresa, the first piece
struck being a "Pfennig," with her bust and arms, date, 1749–65.
The inscription on the obverse of her coins are composed of
the initials of titles, only following the name, they being in
full—*Romanorum Imperatrix, Germania, Hungaria, Bohemia
Regina, Archidux Austria* (R.I.G.H.B.R.A.A.).   A " Heller " of

FIG. 60.—One Kreuzer of Maria Theresa, 1761.

1765–79, bears the Arms alone, while values of $\frac{1}{4}$, $\frac{1}{2}$ and 1
" Kreuzer " bear a bust on obverse and value and date within a
cartouche on reverse.   There are two types of the last three—
one with undraped bust and one with veiled bust.   These pieces
are all small and thick.

FRANCIS I.—The consort of Maria Theresa is represented
by $\frac{1}{2}$ and 1 " Kreuzer," very similar to hers, but bearing his
bust and titles.   They bear the dates 1760–63, co-existing with
the former.

JOSEPH II., both during his mother's life (1765–80) and
later, is represented on copper coins of $\frac{1}{4}$, $\frac{1}{2}$ and 1 " Kreuzer "
values, of the same general type (see *Netherlands*).

FRANCIS II. (last " Holy Roman " Emperor), 1800, $\frac{1}{4}$ " Kr."
Arms and value, $\frac{1}{2}$, 1, 3 and 6 " Kr."   *Obv*. Arms.   *Rev*.
Double-headed Eagle, with value in oval on breast.   Afterwards
as

FRANCIS I. (of the Austrian Empire).   This monarch is
represented by—1807, large pieces of 15 and 30 "Kreuzers

with bust and arms within enclosure of dots or pellets, and with long and elaborate inscriptions, value several times repeated on both sides.   1812, pieces of $\frac{1}{4}$, $\frac{1}{2}$, 1 and 3 "Kreuzers," with bust on *Obv.* and value in ornamental circle on *Rev.* 1816, $\frac{1}{4}$, $\frac{1}{2}$ and 1 "Kreuzer."   *Obv.* Arms in crowned shield

FIG. 61.—One Kreuzer of Francis I., 1816.

FIG. 62.—Three Kreuzers of Francis Joseph I., 1851.

and inscription (as up to the present day), K.K. OESTERREICH-ISCHE SCHEIDEMÜNZE." *Rev.* Value and date in three lines.

FRANCIS JOSEPH I.—1848, 2 "Kreuzers," similar to foregoing series.   1851, $\frac{1}{4}$, $\frac{1}{2}$, 1, 2 and 3 "Kr." *Obv.* Arms and inscription. *Rev.* Value and date. 1858–81, $\frac{5}{10}$, 1 and 4 "Kreuzers" (intrinsic value much reduced), of same type as the preceding.

BURGAU.

(Arms—broad band *l.*, triple cross *r.*)

Initials of titles on coins of Burgau terminate with "— M.B." *Mint marks* G and H.

MARIA THERESA.—1772–7, 1 "Heller" and $\frac{1}{4}$, $\frac{1}{2}$ and 1

"Kreuzer." *Obv.* Arms and ins. *Rev.* Value and date in cartouche.

JOSEPH II.—1781–90, same values, similar type. Also variety of 1 "Kr." without ins. (1771–4).

LEOPOLD II.—1790–2, 1 "Heller" and 1 "Kreuzer." Arms and inscription.

FRANCIS II. (I. of Austria).—1793–1803, 1 "Heller." Arms, no ins. 1793–1805, $\frac{1}{4}$, $\frac{1}{2}$ and 1 "Kr." Arms and ins.

SALZBURG.

(Arms—Lion and two bars.)

1775–1802, "Pfennings" and multiples and "Kreuzers," various types. S-B or SALZBURG.

FERDINAND.—1804, 1 and 2 "Pfennings." *Obv.* Bust. *Rev.* Value and date in diamond.

1804–6, 1 and 2 Pfennings. *Obv.* Bust. *Rev.* EIN or ZWEI PFENNING. 1804–5, 1 "Kreuzer." *Obv.* Bust. *Rev.* Value and date in diamond.

THE TYROL.

(Arms—An Eagle.)

1739, $\frac{1}{2}$ and 1 "Soldo;" Arms. 1809, 1 "Kreuzer" with Arms and GEFURSTETE GRAFSCHAFT TIROL.

GORITZ.

(Arms—Lion on incline and two bars.)

1733 to 1802, Pieces of $\frac{1}{2}$, and 1, 2 and 3 Soldi. *Obv.* Arms. *Rev.* Value and date (various).

KINGDOM OF HUNGARY.

(JOINED TO AUSTRIA IN 1867.)

(Arms.—Four bars *l.*, double cross out of crown on clouds *r.*)

FRANCIS RAGOCZY.—1704–7, 1, 10 and 20 "Poltura," crowned Arms.

MARIA THERESA.—1761–75, $\frac{1}{2}$ and 1 "Greschl," Arms. 1 "Poltura," Bust.

Franz Josef.—1848–9, egy krajczar (1. "Kreuzer"), harom krajczar (3 "Kreuzers"), Arms.   1868, 4 "Kreuzers" (numeral and date in wreath).   *Obv.* Arms.

Fig. 63 – One Kreuzer of Hungary before the Union with Austria, 1848.

Fig. 64.—Four Kreuzers of Hungary after the Union with Austria, 1868.

TRANSYLVANIA.

1763–5.—1 "Greschl," Arms—Head and wings of an Eagle, seven castles below.

BOHEMIA.

(Arms—Lion and two Eagles.)

1759–67, 1 "Groeschl," crowned Arms (in three ovals). 1781–2, 1 "Groeschl," crowned Arms.

AUSTRIAN POLAND.

1774, 1 "Schilling," Austrian Arms crowned in a crowned shield.   1794, 1 and iii "Grossus," Arms above crossed flags. *Rev.* Value and pol.

ITALY.

The same observations which have been made with reference to the inequalities and inconsistencies of the German coinage will apply to that of the entire Italian peninsula, the different parts of which have been divided and sub-divided, united under Republics, independent Monarchies, Principalities, Dukedoms, and the Papacy, or torn asunder by foreign powers, which have imposed their own laws, governors and currency upon the conquered races. This, as history will show, has been going on ever since the dismemberment of the Roman Empire, which fact alone renders the varied modern copper coinage of Europe, few of the pieces being rare, of splendid interest. As I have stated (*see* SPAIN), the oldest copper coins of Europe, not Roman or Byzantine, were those with which the Normans continued the issues of the latter people in

NAPLES AND SICILY,

particularly speaking, those of Count (later, King) Roger, who succeeded his father, Robert Guiscard, the invader and conqueror of Naples from the Byzantines and Sicily from the Saracens.

ROGER.—Coins of 1085–1154 have on *Obv.* the ruler mounted and bearing a standard. *Ins.* ROGERIVS COMES. *Rev.* the Madonna and child with *ins.*, MARIA MATER DNI. Another copper coin of Roger bears a large cross with $\frac{\text{RO} \mid \text{GE}}{\text{CO} \mid \text{ME}}$ lettering in the angles; another, a half figure of the virgin dividing S-M. *Rev.* ROGERIVS DVX. Crowned king in 1129, Roger is represented by a small copper coin bearing ROGERIVS in a circle about "REX" in one line. Roger was succeeded by his son.

WILLIAM I., who coined no copper money.

FIG 65.—Follaro of William II., Norman King of Sicily

WILLIAM II, 1166–89., is designated on his coins by his initial "w," followed by REX II, or DEI GRATIA REX, or other initials. On some of his coins are found a tree or plant, and on others a lion's face. Arabic and Latin inscriptions are also mingled.

TANCRED, 1189–95.—Copper coins bear his name in angles of cross and crowned "T." Also Arabic *ins.* on some.

FREDERICK, 1201–50 (II. of Germany), issued various copper coins, on which he is called ROM. IMPERATOR or REX IER ET SICIL (Jerusalem and Sicily). Only the initial "F" is given for his name. The types are : a Cross, an Eagle, Head, or FR in field.

CONRAD (of Germany), 1250–53.—Coins bear a cross, name, COR or CONRAD, and title.

MANFRED, 1258–66.—One coin *Obv.* "m" surrounded by AYNFR REX. *Rev.* Cross and SICILIE. During the next 150 years there are but few copper coins. Of those which exist the type is almost always of a cross, surrounded by IER ET SIC or SICIL ET IER.

ALFONSO (of Arragon), 1442–58, has left a small copper coin with his head and name on *Obv.*, and the Arragonese and Sicilian Arms quartered on *Rev.*

FERDINAND I (of Arragon), 1458–94.—Copper coins all bear a crowned head with FERDINANDVS REX. *Rev.* A horse with

FIG. 66.—Cavallo of Sicily. Ferdinand I.

EQVITAS REGNI.   Other *Revs.* are more properly medallets.

FIG. 67.—Cinquina of Frederick III., Sicily.

FREDERICK III., 1496–1500.—Coins bear bust or Arms and title, FEDERICVS D G. R. SI. *Rev.* A horse or cross.

LOUIS (XII. of France) has left a small copper coin with his half length figure on *Obv.* with titles and cross, etc., on *Rev.*

CHARLES AND JOHANNA (of Spain), 1516–20.—Copper bears I.C. crowned, or IVSTVS REX around cross, or both.

CHARLES V., 1520–54.—Copper bears bust and titles, CAROLVS V ROM. IMP. *Rev.* Crown or cross and *ins.* Other varieties, IVSTVS REX around cross. *Rev.* PLVS VLTRA around pillars, or REGVM PAX around trophy of arms.

PHILIP II., 1554–98.—Copper, *Obv.* Bust and titles. *Rev.* 1 " Cavallo," cross ; 2 " Cavalli," crown ; 4 "Cavalli," cornucopia, etc.

PHILIP III., 1598–1621.—Various types, usually bust, always titles. *Revs.* the usual Sicilian types, cross, crown, cornucopia, a plant, or the Golden Fleece (a lamb), various inscriptions.

PHILIP IV, 1621–65.—Same types, also Lion and Castle and Arms, and PVBLICA COMMODITAS filling field.

HENRY OF LORRAINE, 1648.—S.P.Q.N. in crowned shield, surrounded by name and title.

CHARLES II., 1665–1700.—*Obv.* Bust and titles. *Rev.* Usual

FIG. 68.—Two Tornesi of Sicily   Charles II. (of Spain), (16)82.

types of predecessors, also crowned Eagle.

PHILIP V., 1701–8.—*Obv.* Bust and titles. *Rev.* Arms, Fleece, or *ins.*

VICTOR AMADEUS, 1713–20.—1 " Tornese." *Obv.* Eagle, etc. *Rev.* PVBLICA-COMMO-DITAS.

CHARLES III. (VI. of Germany), 1720–34.—1 and 2 " Tornesi." *Obv.* Eagle. *Rev.* VT FACILIUS. Same *Rev.* VT COMMODIVS, all *cast.*

CARLOS OF BOURBON, 1734–59 (title of Charles III. also).— *Obv.* Eagle or bust and titles ; various *Revs.*

FERDINAND IV., 1759–1825.—This monarch changed his number of succession at least four times. From 1776 to 1799 he is F. IV; 1802–16, F. III; 1816, F. IV again; 1819, F. I. His coins all bear his titles with Eagle or bust on *Obv*. *Rev*. Various types, value and date, castle, cross, grapes, cornucopiæ, etc. Values—Grani, Cavalli, and Tornese. There is a change

FIG. 69.—Four Cavalli of Ferdinand IV. (1st).

FIG. 70.—Five Tornesi of Sicily (cast coin of 1797).

FIG. 71.— One Grano of Ferdinand III. (1st).

of type of coins with that of title. The bust of 1814–15 is crowned, others flowing hair.

GIOACCHINO NAP(oleon) (Joachim Murat), 1808–15, deposed Ferdinand during this period. Copper coins, 2 and 3 "Grani," and 5 and 10 "Centesimi" with bust and titles. Values and date on *Rev*.

FRANCIS I., 1825–30.—1, 2, 5, and 10 "Tornesi." *Obv*. Bust and titles. *Rev*. Value under large crown, and date.

FERDINAND II., 1831–59.—$\frac{1}{2}$, 1, 1$\frac{1}{2}$, 2, 3, 5 and 10 "Tornesi." Same general type as preceding.

Francis II., 1859.—2 and 10 "Tornesi." *Obv.* Bust and titles. *Rev.* Value under *fleur de lis.*

Fig. 72.—Half Tornese of Ferdinand II.

Fig. .73—Reverse of Ten Tornese of Ferdinand II. (Type of series.)

NEAPOLITAN REPUBLIC.

(1799.)

Of this short-lived institution there are to be found pieces of 4 and 6 "Tornese," bearing a *fasces* and REPVBBLICA NAPOLITANA.

ORBETELLO.

1782–98. Pieces of I, II and IIII "Quattrini." *Obv.* Bust

Fig. 74.—Quattrino of Orbetello, 1782.

and titles of Ferdinand IV. *Rev.* REALI PRESIDII, and value under crown.

PALMA NUOVA.

Napoleon I., 1814.—25 and 50 "Centesimi." *Obv.* MONTE D'ASSED-PALMA. *Rev.* Value surrounded by NAPOLEONE IMPE. E. RE.

THE STATES OF THE CHURCH.
(PAPAL STATES.)

The coins struck by the Papal authorities of Rome are not difficult to classify, seeing that almost all bear the same *Obv.* type—the Arms of the sovereign Pontiff surrounded by his title and the date of his Pontificate. The Roman series is of course the principal, but there are coins of various localities, outside, bearing the Papal Arms, which must not be confounded with them. I shall note the difference. The *Revs.* of the earlier Papal coins are usually occupied by figures of the Saints, Peter or Paul, or the holy gateway; the later *Revs.* bear merely value and date, the values being in " Quat-

FIG. 75.—Half Baiocco of Benedict XIV., 1750. (Type.)

FIG. 76.—Two-and-a-half Baiocchi, Papal. St. Peter type (halo omitted by mischance

trini " and " Baiocchi," and the word ROMANI to indicate their origin.

The "Papal Arms" consist of the *personal* Arms ot the reigning Pope on a shield surmounted by the Tiara and Keys

Fɪɢ. 77.—Baiocco of Papal States during Interregnum of 1740.   "Sede Vacante.

Fɪɢ. 78.—Two Baiocchi of Pius IX., with Arms.   General type of series.

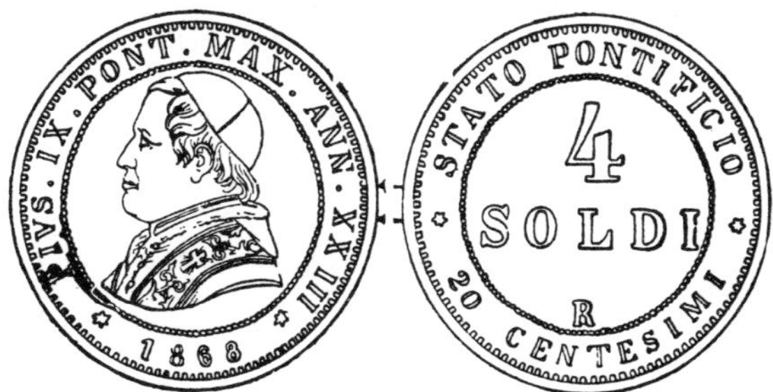

Fɪɢ. 79.—Four Soldi of Pius IX.   (Last Papal coins.)

of St. Peter.   When coins are issued during a vacancy the Arms are those of the senior Cardinal surmounted by his hat, and above all the Keys under an umbrella or canopy.   The inscription will then be SEDE VACANTE, as in 1623 and 1740. The last coinage of the Papal States was under the late Pius IX., who, after a series of the usual type, issued in 1866–9 pieces of 1 "Centesimi" and $\frac{1}{2}$, 1, 2 and 4 "Soldi," with his bust upon the *Obv.* The full inscription on a Papal coin following the name of the Pope is PONTIFEX MAXIMUS. ANNO (year in Roman numerals). The foregoing and a list of the Popes for the last three hundred years will suffice to identify any coin of the series.

CLEMENT VIII., 1592–1605.	INNOCENT XIII., 1721–24.
PAUL V., 1605–21.	BENEDICT XIII., 1724–30.
GREGORY XV., 1621–23.	CLEMENT XII., 1730–40.
Vacancy, 1623.	*Vacancy*, 1740.
URBAN VIII., 1623–44.	BENEDICT XIV., 1740–58.
INNOCENT X., 1644–55.	CLEMENT XIII., 1758–69.
ALEXANDER VII., 1655–67.	CLEMENT XIV., 1769–74.
CLEMENT IX., 1667–69.	PIUS VI., 1775–99.
CLEMENT X., 1670–76.	PIUS VII., 1800–23.
INNOCENT XI., 1676–89.	LEO XII., 1823–29.
ALEXANDER VIII., 1689–91.	PIUS VIII., 1829–30.
INNOCENT XII., 1691–1700.	GREGORY XVI., 1831–46.
CLEMENT XI., 1700–21.	PIUS IX., 1846–78.

The present Pope, Leo XIII., has issued no copper coins.

THE ITALIAN PROVINCES.

(Names usually appear on coins.)

There being absolutely no sequence or connection to be observed in any of the series of coins belonging to these territories, the only possible manner of classifying them is by alphabetical order. Two types however are very common, and are nearly alike for all places with sole exception of the name given. They are : (1) *Obv.* Head of the Madonna surrounded by SANCTA DEI, GENETRIX. *Rev.* Value and name of locality surrounded by name, title, and apostolical date of Pope (Pius VI.); date below. (2) *Obv.* Bust of St. Peter holding keys, surrounded by S. P. APOSTOLORVM PRINCEPS. *Rev.* Value, place and date.

ANCONA.—1796, 1 and 2 "Baiocchi." Arms and name expressed, 2$\frac{1}{2}$ Bai. Bust of St. Peter. 1798–9, 2 "Bai." Republic, *fasces*, 1849, 1 "Baiocco," cast brass. *Obv. Fasces* and REPUBBLICA ROMANA. *Rev.* Value and mint mark "A" (ncona).

AQUILA (Arms—an Eagle).—1484–92, " Quattrino," Innocent VIII. (Pope). *Obv.* Keys. *Rev.* Eagle. 1483–98, "Quattrino," Charles VIII. (France). *Obv.* Arms. *Rev.* Cross.

ASCOLI.—1492–1503, "Quattrino," Alexander VI. (Pope). *Obv.* Arms. *Rev.* Castle and DE-A-SCULO. Pius VI., 1797, various values with Arms. Name on *Rev.*

BOLOGNA.—Arms—a Lion (usually supporting a standard) and motto BONONIA DOCET (Bologna Teaches) usually appear

FIG. 80.—Quattrino of Bologna, 1749.

on coins of Bologna, whether of Papal or civic origin. The small local copper coin is called a " Bolognino."

CHIETI.—Few coins bear a cross and device CIVITAS TEATINA (City of Chieti).

CIVITA VECCHIA.—1796–7, $2\frac{1}{2}$ and 5 " Baiocchi " of Papal type. (Pius VI.)

CLITUNNO.—1798–9, " Baiocco " of Roman Republic, with *fasces*.

ETRURIA.—1803–7, " Quattrino," $\frac{1}{2}$, 1, and 2 "Soldi " of Maria Louisa and Charles Louis. Arms and *ins*. 1818, 2 "Soldi " of Ferdinand III. Arms and *ins*.

FANO.—$2\frac{1}{2}$ and 5 " Baiocchi " of Pius VI., 1775–99. Papal type.

FERMO.—*Same.* Also coins of Roman Republic, 1798–9.

FERRARA.—" Quattrinos " with *Obv.* St. George and Dragon. $\frac{1}{2}$ " Baiocchi " of several Popes.

FULIGNO.—Papal coins of Pius VI., 1775–99.

GENOA.—Republic of 1814. 2 and 4 Soldi. *Obv.* Arms of Savoy with "RESPUBLICA GENUENSIS." *Rev.* of 4 Soldi St. George and "EX PROBITATE ROBUR." *Rev.* of 2 Soldi, The Immaculate Conception and "SUB TUUM PRESIDIUM." Both quite scarce.

GUBBIO (*Latin*, Eugubia).—Papal coins from Clement XII. to Pius VI., and under Roman Republic.

LOMBARDY-VENICE, 1822–62.—Coins bear Austrian crown, REGNO LOMBARDO-VENETO.   Value in centesimi.

FIG. 81.—Three Centesimi of Austrian Italy (Lombardy Venice), 1846.

LUCCA.—1555–66, "Quattrino" of Otto (German Emperor), OTTO IMPERATOR around "L." 1682, "Bolognino" with figure of St. Peter and L-V-C-A.   1717–90, "Bolognino." Arms with a lion.   *Rev.* St. Peter.   1756–90, 1 and 2 "Soldi." *Obv.* Arms.   *Rev.* Value, etc.   Charles Louis, 1824–47, coins of several types and values with name, titles, etc.   Arms a *fleur de lis*.

LUCCA AND PIOMBINO.—Felix and Elisa, 1806–14, 3 and 5 "Centesimi."   Busts of both with names and titles.

MANTUA.—Coins, "Sesino" and "Soldo."   Arms a cross

FIG. 82.—Sesino of Mantua.

or rayed sun; also Austrian Arms.   Name given on all—MANTOVA.   Under Austrian rule till federation of Italy.

MACERETA.—1797–8, 5 "Bai."   The Virgin and SANCTA DEI GENETRIX.   1798–9, "Quattrino" and ½ "Bai," Roman Republic, *fasces*.

MASSA-CARRARA.—1790–1828, "Quattrino," 1 and 2 "Soldi" of Maria Beatrix.   Arms and *ins.*   *Rev.* Value, etc.

MATELICA.—1775–99.   Papal types of Pius VII.

MILAN.—Arms, an undulating serpent, upright in shield. All coins easily identifiable through arms or name MEDIOLANUM. Coins of Philips III., IV. and V., and Charles II. and III. of Spain, after which of Maria Theresa. Values in "Quattrinos," "Sesinos" and "Soldos," or parts thereof.

MIRANDOLA.—"Sesinos," 15th, 16th, and 17th centuries. *Obv.* Arms or bust of Ruler. *Rev.* MIRANDOLA, etc.

MODENA (*Latin* MUTINA).—Arms, an eagle. 18th century, "Sesino" with Arms or Bust of reigning duke, also Bust

FIG. 83.—Sesino of Modena.

and Arms. *Rev.* MVTIN-SESIN, variety with *fleur de lis*. "Soldo" and "Bolognino," 1783, with Arms.

MONACO.—Pieces of 8 "Denarii" of Antonius, 1720, and Honore III., 1734-9. *Obv.* Initial crowned. *Rev.* A saint. Honore V., 1819-41, 5 "Centimes" and 1 "Decime" of French type. *Obv.* Bust and title. *Rev.* Value and date in wreath.

MONTALTO.—1775-99, $2\frac{1}{2}$ and 5 "Baiocchi," Pius VI. Papal types. St. Peter or Virgin.

PARMA.—1586-92, 11 "Quattrini" of Alexander Farnese. *Obv.* Bust surrounded by AL. F SPECVLATOR. *Rev.* "11—P." 1622-46, "Quattrino," "Sesino" and "Soldo" of Edward. *Obv.* Crowned Arms. *Rev.* Saint Hilarius. Other coins from Ranutius II. (1646) to Maria Louisa (also of Piacenza and Guastalla), ending 1824, all bear Arms on *Obv.*

PERGOLA.—Papal coins of Pius VI., 1775-99, and under Roman Republic, 1798-9, *fasces* type with name.

PERUGIA.—"Quattrino" of Republic, 1260-1506. *Obv.* A large "P." *Rev.* SANCTUS ERCULANUS. Papal copper of Pius VI., and 2 "Baiocchi" of Roman Republic similar to others.

PIEDMONT.—2 "Soldi" of the Republic of 1801. *Obv.*

Triangle in wreath, LIBERTA*EGUAGLIANZA*. *Rev.* NAZIONE PIEMONTESE around "*Soldi due*" in script.

RAGUSA.—Follaro, 15th century. *Obv.* Head and RACVSII MONETA. *Rev.* Castle and RACVSII CIVITAS. "Soldo," 1729–95, *Obv.* Saint standing. *Rev.* Similar to foregoing. 6 "Soldi," 1795–6, same type. DEVS REFVGI, etc.

RAVENNA.—Papal coins of Benedict XIV. Arms on

FIG. 84.—Quattrino of Ravenna, Benedict XIV., Pope

Obv., with Arms of city (a fir cone). A saint or value on *Rev* RAV or RAVENNA always given.

RONCIGLIONE.—Varieties of 3 "Baiocchi," 1799. *Obv* the Madonna. *Rev. Ins.* or value.

SAN MARINO.—(Independent Republic). 5 "Centesimi," 1864–9; 10 "Cent.," 1875. *Obv.* Arms, three flaming beacon towers. *Rev.* Value.

SAN SEVERINO.—Papal coins of Pius VI., giving name.

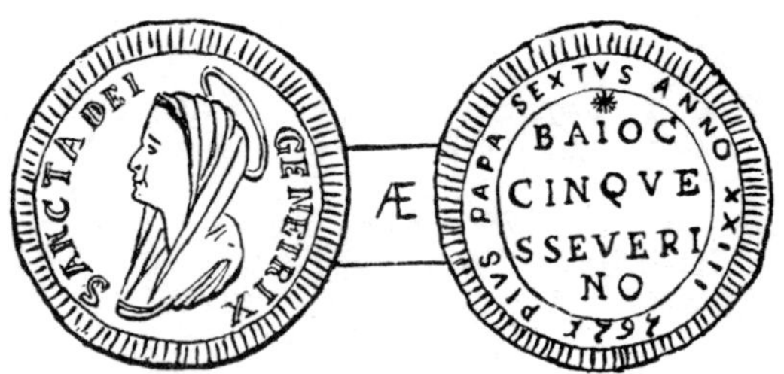

FIG. 85.—Five Baiocchi of San Severino. Pope Pius VI., 1797. (Virgin type.

SPOLETO.—1797, Pius VI., 5 "Baiocchi." The Madonna, SANCTA DEI GENETRIX.

TERNI.—1797, The same.

TIVOLI.—1797, The same.

URBINO.—"Quattrinos," 1500–8, Guido Uboldo I. *Obv.* Bust. *Rev.* Arms and FIDES SPES CARITAS. G. U. II., 1538–74, "GII" crowned. Francis Maria II. *Obv.* A tree, name and title (VRBINO DVX). *Rev.* An Eagle.

VITERBO.—Papal coins of Pius VI., 1775–99.

ROMAN REPUBLICS.

1.—1798–9, ½, 1 and 2 "Baiocchi." *Obv. Fasces* and REPUBLICA ROMANA. *Rev.* Value within wreath.

2.—1849, ½, 1 and 3 "Baiocchi." *Obv.* An Eagle and DIO E POPOLO. *Rev.* Value, date, etc.

SARDINIA.

Under Spain, 1 and 3 "Cagliarese," Philip IV. and Charles II. Same under Charles VI. of Germany. Type.—*Obv* Bust and titles. *Rev.* A cross with *ins.*

THE KINGDOM.—1773–96, Victor Amadeus III., 2 "Denarii." *Obv.* Crowned knot and date. *Rev.* Cross surrounded by *ins.* ½ and 1 "Soldo." "*V.A.*" *script monogram.* 5 "Soldi." *Obv.* Bust and *ins.* *Rev.* St. Mauritus. Charles Emanuel IV., 1796–1802, 2 "Denarii," previous type. 1 "Soldo," *script monogram* "*E.C.E.*" and cross. "7 Soldi, 6 Denarii." *Obv.* Bust and titles. *Rev.* Arms (an Eagle) in oval, and value, "SOL 7.6." Charles Felix, 1826, 1, 3 and 5

FIG. 86.—Five Centesimi of Charles Felix, Sardinia, 1826.

"Centesimi." *Obv.* Crowned Eagle in wreath. *Rev.* Value, date and *ins.* Charles Albert, 1842, 1, 3 and 5 "Centesimi." *Obv.* Crowned Arms (four negroes' heads in angles of cross). *Rev.* Value and date.

CORSICA.

This little island, besides possessing the glory of having produced the great Napoleon, has a little numismatic history of its own. In 1736 coins were struck by the celebrated German adventurer Baron Neuhoff, who enjoyed a brief and

FIG. 87.—Five Soldi of King Theodore of Corsica, 1736.

disastrous rule as Theodore I. His issues in copper were pieces of 2 and 5 "Soldi." *Obv.* T. R. crowned (Theodorus Rex). *Rev.* Value within circle, surrounded by inscription PRO · BONO · PUBLICO · RO · CE or abbreviation thereof. The patriot Pascal Paoli is represented by first a "Soldo" of 1768. *Obv.* Liberty cap on pole. *Rev.* Value, etc. 2 and 4 "Soldi" of 1763–6 bear *Obv.* a crowned shield bearing the head of a

FIG. 88.—Four Soldi of Pascal Paoli, Corsica.

negro and supported by two half figures grasping bludgeons. *Rev.* Value and date within a wreath.

TUSCANY.

Copper coins all bear Arms, name and titles of ruler. Values, "Quattrini" and "Soldi." Peter Leopold, 1765–90. Ferdinand III., 1790–1824. Leopold II., 1824–59. Finally pieces of 1, 2 and 5 "Centimes." *Obv.* Arms of Italy as at present, surrounded by VITTORIO EMANUELE RE ELETTO. *Rev.* Value and date, 1859–61, surrounded by GOVERNO DELLA TOSCANA.

VENICE.

None of the Venetian Ducal copper coins are dated, so that their age can only be approximated by the name of the Doge appearing thereon, from early in the thirteenth century, down. The types are as follows : "Bagattino," *Obv.* A head or lion. *Rev.* A cross. "Quattrino," *Obv.* A lion surrounded by SANCTVS MARCVS VENETVS. *Rev.* A cross surrounded by name and title of Doge (DVX). ½ and 1 "Soldo," *Obv.* The Doge

FIG. 89—Soldo of Venetian Republic. Doge Aloysius Mocenigo, 1570-1577.

kneeling, holding standard before Lion of St. Mark surrounded by name, value in exergue, 6 or 12. *Rev.* Standing figure of St. Mark surrounded by DEFENS NOSTER.

UNCLASSIFIABLE.—"Bagattino." *Obv.* The Madonna, with R.C.L.A. (Regina Cœli Laetare Alleluia). *Rev.* Lion in square. ½ "Soldo." *Obv.* Same. *Rev.* SAN. MARC. VEN around bust.

PROVISIONAL GOVERNMENT (Revolution of 1848–9).—1, 3 and 5 "Centesimi." *Obv.* Lion of St. Mark, GOVERNO PROVISORIO DI VENEZIA. *Rev.* Value, CENTESIMI DI LIRA CORRENTE, and date.

ITALY (UNITED.)

REPUBLIC.—1802–5, 1, 2 and 5 "Denarii." *Obv.* 1, 2 or 5 ears of corn, date AN II. *Rev.* Value. "Centesimo," ½ and 1 "Soldo," 1804, *Obv.* Scales and palm branch, (varieties).

NAPOLEON I.—1805–14, 1, 2 and 3 "Centesimi." Type— *Obv.* Head surrounded by NAPOLEONE IMPERATORE E. RE., date below bust. *Rev.* A crown, REGNO D'ITALIA above, value

below.   There are several varieties of head employed.   The
first coinage, of 1806, is quite scarce.

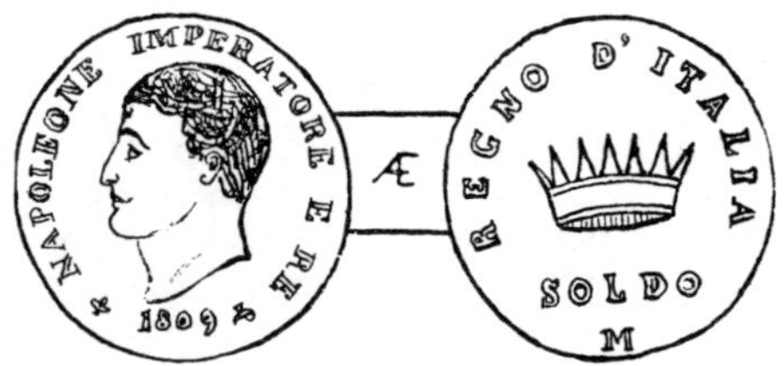

FIG. 90.—Soldo of Napoleon Bonaparte as King of Italy, 1809.

VICTOR EMANUEL II.—1861–78, 1, 2, 5 and 10 "Centesimi."

FIG. 91.—Ten Centesimi of Victor Emanuel II., 1862.

Obv. Head and VITTORIO EMANUELE II RE D'ITALIA.   *Rev.*
Value and date in wreath.

HUMBERT I.—1878, 1 and 2 "Centesimi."   Struck as pat-
terns.   Scarce.

THE NETHERLANDS.

The above in its original sense is a general term, probably best understood by its translation,—the " Low Countries," or *Pays Bas* (French), comprising the modern kingdoms of Holland and part of Belgium, which latter is the " Flanders " of Marlborough's campaigns. For centuries the battle-field of Europe, the Netherlands have enjoyed the usual fortune of such a position in divisions and sub-divisions innumerable, with an occasional tyranny of some foreign power to relieve the monotony of self-government. Hence, as in other cases elsewhere mentioned, in default of other means of classifying them, localities are given in alphabetical order. The copper coinage of the Netherlands appears to have been introduced by the Emperor, Charles V., whose son, Philip II. of Spain, was the first to strike a liberal coinage of copper in all parts. I give the more important provinces first.

BRABANT.—Of Charles V., 1506–56, there are " Mytes " with a crowned " K " or Arms and titles. A half " Liard " of 1543–56 bears *Obv.* Bust and title. *Rev.* a Lion. Philip II., 1556–98, copper in " Mytes," " Liards," and halves. *Obv.* Bust or cross. *Rev.* Arms or cross. Title of ruler whose name is given, ARCHIDVX AVST(ria) DVX BVRG, BRAB(ant). Albert and Elizabeth, 1598–1621, ½ " Liard," Æ crowned ; ½ and 1 " Liard,"

FIG. 92.—Liard of Brabant. Philip IV. (of Spain). (Type.)

Arms and *ins.* *Rev.* a Cross. Philip IV., type. *Obv.* Cross of Arms and *ins.* *Rev.* Spanish Arms and remainder of title. Charles II., 1665–1700, same type. Philip V., 1700–12, 1 and 2 " Liards," same type. 2 " Liards." *Obv.* Bust and titles. *Rev.* Arms and continuation of titles. Maximilian, 1700–12 ; Emanuel, 1712–15, " Liards." *Obv.* Bust or Arms and *ins.*

Charles VI., 1712–16, "Liard." *Obv.* Bust. *Rev.* Crowned initials. The coins of the Austrian rulers, Maria Theresa, 1740–80; Joseph II., 1780–90; Leopold II., 1791–2, and

FIG. 93.—Liard of the Austrian Netherlands. Joseph II., 1789.

Francis II., 1792–7, are all of one type. *Obv.* Bust of sovereign with name and titles. *Rev.* AD-USUM-BELGII-AUSTR(ii) and date within wreath. Values, 1 and 2 "Liards." The insurgents

FIG. 94.—Liard of the Belgian Confederation, 1790.

of 1790 struck copper 1 and 2 "Liards." *Obv.* Lion holding hat on pole. *Rev.* AD-USUM FŒDERATI-BELGII-1790.

FLANDERS.—1545–52, "Doit." *Obv.* Bust and *ins.* *Rev.* A lion. Philip II., Albert and Elizabeth, Philip IV., and Charles II. are represented by coins similar to those of Brabant. The *Rev.* legend is however ARCHID · AVS · DVX · BVRG C . FL (*Comes Flanders*). A "Liard" of Maximilian Emanuel, 1712–15, bears *Obv.* Bust and *ins.* *Rev. Script mon,* M.E. "Liard" of Charles VI., 1712–15, *Obv.* Bust. *Rev.* three C's, crowned.

NETHERLAND PROVINCES.

(16th, 17th and 18th Centuries.)

The copper coinage of these States is expressed in "Mytes," "Doits," and "Liards," with *fractions* and *multiples.* The various types, whether of the Spanish occupation or otherwise, are distinguishable by either the Arms or name of the province, usually both in conjunction. Want of space forbids the enumeration of all known varieties, the list of which is, by the enormous issues of private *jetons* or tokens, and the issues of ecclesiastical dignitaries, rendered almost interminable. The " Doit " is by far the most common and easily obtainable coin. The following are leading characteristics :—

HOLLAND (*Hollandia*).—Arms, a Lion in wicket en-

FIG. 95.—Doit of Holland, 1769. (Type of other provinces.)

closure. Varieties, a Cross or female figure in wicket (name or province on coins of this series often fills entire field of *Rev.*).

FRIESLAND (*Frisia*).—Arms, two Lions one above the other in crowned shield.

GELDERLAND (*Gelriæ*).—Arms, two lions, facing in halves of crowned shield. Motto, IN DEO EST SPES NOSTRA.

GRONINGEN.—Arms, Double-headed Eagle, or same quartered with four oblique rows of small hearts. *Rev.* GRONINGA, or GRON-EN-OMMEL.

OVERYSSEL (*Transisulania*).—Arms, a Lion rampant on a wavy bar. Motto, VIGILATE ET ORATE.

UTRECHT (*Trajectum*, or STAD UTRECHT).—Arms, a crowned shield supported by two lions.

FIG. 96.—Doit of Zealand, 1766. (Type of other provinces.

WEST FRIESLAND (*West Frisiæ*).—Arms, two lions one above the other, heads *l.*

ZEALAND (*Zelandia*). — Arms, a Lion emerging from water. Motto, LUCTOR ET EMERGO.

DUTCH AND FLEMISH LOCAL ISSUES.

(Alphabetically.)

ALOST.—1833, 1, 5, and 25 "Centimes," MONNAIE FICTIVE.

ANHOLT.—"Doits" with CIV-ITAS-ANH, or CVS, ANH.

ANVERS (*Antwerp*), 1814.—Obsidional money of Napoleon I. and of Louis XVIII., 5 and 10 "Centimes," crowned N or crowned double L.

ARNHEM.—"Doit." *Rev.* Arms.

ARTOIS.—"Liards" of Philip II. (15)82–96 and Philip IV., 1636–9. *Obv.* Bust. *Rev.* Arms (nearly the same as those of Brabant, on a single shield.

BATTENBURG. \ John II., 1588–1617, ½ and 1 "Liard :" *Obv.* Bust, IOES COMES, etc. *Rev.* Arms. "Liard" with Arms on both sides.

BRONKHORST. \ Justus Maximilian, 1617–67, 4 "Mytes," ½ and 1 "Liard" several types. All bear Arms and names.

GRONSFELD. | City, ½ Liard. *Obv.* Arms. *Rev.* BAT-ENBVR-GVM, or CIVITATIS BAT.

BOMMEL.—"Doit," Lion holding sword. *Rev.* SALT-BOM-EL.

CAMBRAY.—Ludwig A. Berlaimont, 1570-96. I, II, and VI "Deniers." *Obv.* Arms. *Rev.* I, three lions in shield ; II, Cross ; VI, L-O-Y-S in angles of Cross.

CAMPEN.—Arms, a Lion. *Rev.* usually a Castle with CAM-PEN or CAM-PEN-SIS.

DAVENTER.—Arms, an Eagle. DAVEN or DA-VEN-TRIA.

ELBURG.—Arms, three-towered Castle. *Rev.* MONETA-ECCLES-ELBVRG.

GHENT (*Gana*).—Arms a Lion *rampant.* Coins usually bear name. The 4 "Mytes" of 1584 has a crowned "G," the VI "Mytes" of (15)83-4, S.P.Q.G. on *Reverse.*

FIG. 97.—Six "Mytes" of Ghent.

GORCUM.—"Doit" with Arms and GORC-IN-HOLL.

HUESSEN (*Huissen*).—"Doits," Arms and name.

LEYDEN.—Arms, crossed Keys, ½ "Stuber" (15)74, with ENDE-SALICHT-LEYDEN.

LILLE.—Siege pieces of 1708, V, X and XX SOLS. PRO-DEFENSIONE-VRBIS-ET-PATRIE.

LOOS.—Pieces of XII "Sous" of Ernst, 1583–94, and "Liards" of Ferdinand, 1612–50. Bust or Arms.

MAESTRICHT.—Siege pieces of 1579. ½, I, II, VIII, XII, XVI, XXIIII and XXXX "Sols." *Obv.* Arms, a five-pointed Star and date. *Rev.* TRAJECTO AB HISPANIO OBSESSO.

NAMUR.—½ and 1 "Liard" of Philip II., 1578–9. Usual type.

NYMWEGEN.—"Doits." Female in wicket or holding shield. *Rev.* NOV-IMA-GVM.

RECKHEIM (*Trarechem*).—Coins bear Arms and name in full or abbreviated.

ROERMOND.—Spanish rulers. "Doits," and "Liards" with Arms, a Lion and *fleur de lis.*

ST. BERNARD.—1, 5, and 25 "Centimes." MONNAIE FICTIVE, 1833.

STAVENSWERTH.—Arms, a Lion. "Doits" with SST-INSV-LA, or SST-WERTE-CVSA.

TOURNAY (*Tornaco*).—½ and 1 "Liard" (Spanish rule), usual types. 1709, siege pieces of 2 and 8 "Petards."

VILVORDE.—Same as St. Bernard.

ZUTPHEN.—Arms, Lion *rampant* over cross. "Doits" with ZVTPHANENSIS or similar.

ZWOLLE.—"Doits" with ZW-OLLÆ, etc.

THE KINGDOM OF HOLLAND.
(KONINGRIJK DER NEDERLANDEN).

From 1815 to 1877 the type of coinage is the same, covering reigns of Williams I. 1815–40; II., 1840–49; III., 1849. The *Obv.* of cent and half-cent pieces is a large W crowned,

Fig. 98.—One Cent, William III., 1863.

Fig. 99.—Two and a half Cents, William III., 1884.

dividing date. *Rev.* Arms crowned and dividing value. 1877–86, ½, 1, and 2½ cents bear the Arms in a circle surrounded by *ins.* as above. *Rev.* The value within a wreath.

THE KINGDOM OF BELGIUM

Formed part of the kingdom of the Netherlands until 1831, prior to which the coinage as described above was the same, with the addition of the letter "B" as a mint mark for Brussels, only. In 1832 was commenced the issue of the beautiful coins still in use. The *Obv.* bears the Belgian Lion seated

Fig. 100.—Five Centimes of Leopold I.

guarding a tablet inscribed CONSTITUTION BELGE, 1831. Above is the motto L'UNION FAIT LA FORCE, in exergue the value. *Rev.* An ornate script L crowned, with title of monarch surrounding, date below.   Issues—

LEOPOLD I., 1831–65, 1, 2, 5 and 10 "Centimes."   Also on marriage of the Duke of Brabant, his son, a special piece of 10 "Centimes."   *Obv.* His own head.   *Rev.* Heads of the young Duke and Duchess.

LEOPOLD II., 1865, 1 and 2 " Centime " pieces only.

LIEGE.—There has been a large copper coinage in this Flemish town, emanating principally from ecclesiastical sources, here being the seat of a bishopric.   The Arms are usually Lions

FIG. 101.—Liard of Liege.   Arms of the Bavarian Bishop, John Theodore Charles.

quartered with diamond-shaped lozenges (Bavarian).   Frequently the bust of St. Lambertus is employed, and often five shields in the form of a cross, with the date in angles.   The name of the city appears as LEODENSIS, LEOD, or LEO.   The Princes and Bishops who issued coins during three hundred years were,—

George, 1563–80 (of Austria).
Gerard von Groesbeck, 1563–80.
Ernst, 1580–1612 (House of Bavaria).
Ferdinand, 1612–50.
Maxmilian Henry, 1650–88.
John Ludwig von Elderen, 1688–94.
Josef Clement (Bavaria), 1694–1723.
George Ludwig von Berghes, 1724–43.
Cornelius von Berghes, 1738–44.
John Theodore, 1744–63.
Sede Vacante, 1688, 1694, 1724.

GRAND DUCHY OF LUXEMBURG.

(Arms—A Lion *rampant*).

MARIA THERESA, 1740–80. —Types : Bust, AD USUM DUCATOS LUXEM. "*M. T.*," *script mon.* or crowned Arms, " Liards," halves and " Sols."

JOSEPH II., 1765–90.—Crowned Arms or II J, J II, *monogram*. " Liards " and " Sols."

LEOPOLD, 1790–92.—Crowned Arms.   " Sols."

WILLIAM III., 1849–70.—Pieces of $2\frac{1}{2}$, 5, and 10 "Centimes." *Obv.* Crowned Arms surrounded by GRAND-DUCHÉ DE LUXEMBOURG.   *Rev.* Value and date within wreath.

RUSSIA.

The copper coinage of Russia is of Asiatic origin on the one hand, while on the other the use of *plate* money was evidently borrowed from her Scandinavian neighbours for a while, and pieces of stamped leather passed as small currency during a long period.   There are certain old pieces recognised to have been current in Russia prior to the time of Peter the Great, but the modern or Regal series had its origin in his reign. The Arms of Russia are a double-headed eagle with sceptre in left talon and orb in right, with a shield depicting St. George and the dragon, upon its breast.   Both heads are crowned separately and are surmounted by a third and larger crown. On the earliest coins the figure of St. George often appears alone.   The piece of $\frac{1}{4}$ Kopeck is called a " POLUSKA," that of $\frac{1}{2}$ a " DENGA."

The various series, to date, are as follows,—

PETER I.— 1689–1725 $\frac{1}{4}$, $\frac{1}{2}$ and 1 Kopeck.   *Obv.* St. George

FIG. 102.—A Kopeck of Peter the Great.

and Russian *ins.* *Rev.* Value surrounded by *ins.* 1723–5, 5 Kopecks. *Obv.* Arms in small circle surrounded by five dots. *Rev.* an outlined cross containing value and date.

FIG. 103.—Five Kopecks of Peter II.

CATHERINE I.—1725–7, 1 Kopeck, St. George. 5 Kopecks, like foregoing.

PETER II.—1727–30, 1 Kopeck, St. George. 5 Kopecks, like foregoing.

FIG. 104. – Denga or ½ Kopeck of Empress Anne

ANNA.—1730–40, ¼ and ½ Kopeck. *Obv.* Arms. *Rev.* Value and date.

IVAN VI.—1740–1, Same as last. (The baby Czar who reigned one year.)

ELISABETH I.—1743–54, ¼ and ½ Kopeck, same as last. 1755–7, 1 Kopeck, "*E.P.*," *script*, and eagle above clouds and date. *Rev.* same and value. 1757–61, ¼, ½ and 1 Kopeck. *Obv.* St. George, value on scroll. *Rev. Script mon.* "*E.E. P.P.*" and date. 1757–62, 2 Kopecks, 2 *var.* value on scroll and value above. 5 Kopecks, 2 *var. Obv.* St. George, and *Obv.* Arms.

Fig. 105.—Two Kopecks of Elisabeth.

PETER III.—1762, 1, 2, 4, and 10 Kopecks. *Obv.* St. George. *Rev.* Value and date in four lines over military trophy.

Fig. 106.—Two Kopecks of Catherine II., 1790.

Fig. 107.—Five Kopecks of Catherine II.   Reverse same as Two Kopeck piece.

CATHERINE II.—1762-76, ¼, ½, 1, and 2 Kopecks. *Obv.* St. George. *Rev. Script monogram "I.E."* and date in wreath. 5 Kopecks, Arms and same *Rev.*

PAUL I.—1796-1801, ¼, ½, 1, and 2 Kopecks. *Obv.* Crowned II over I. *Rev.* Value and date.

FIG. 108.—Kopeck of Paul I.

ALEXANDER I.—1803-10, *First coinage,* ¼, ½, 1, 2, and 5 Kopecks. *Obv.* Arms in circular band. *Rev.* Value and date in same. *Second coinage,* 1810-25, ½, 1, and 2 Kopecks. *Obv.* Arms and date. *Rev.* Value in wreath, crowned.

NICHOLAS I.—1825-55, ½, 1, and 2 Kopecks as in previous reign. *Second coinage,* 1830-39, 1, 2, 5, and 10 Kopecks.

FIG. 109.—Ten Kopecks of Nicholas I. (Second coinage.)

Obv. Double-headed eagle with outstretched wings, holding torch and thunder-bolt *l*, wreath *r*, date below. *Rev.* Value. *Third coinage,* 1839-48, ¼, ½, 1, 2, and 3 Kopecks, *script*

"*H.*" crowned, over I. *Rev.* Value and date, four lines. *Fourth coinage*, 1849–60, ¼, ½, and 1 Kopeck, "H." crowned

FIG. 110.—Kopeck of Nicholas I. (Third coinage.)

over I. *Rev.* Value and date, 2, 3, and 5 Kopecks. *Obv.* Arms.

ALEXANDER II.—1855–61, ¼, ½, and 1 Kopeck, *script* "*A*" crowned over II, 1855–65, 2, 3, and 5 Kopecks like fore-

FIG. 111.—Kopeck of Alexander II.

going. *Second coinage*, 1867–81, ¼ and ½ Kopeck, "A II," crowned, milled edges. 1867–81, 1, 2, 3, and 5 Kopecks.

FIG. 112.—Five Kopecks of Alexander II., 1868.

Arms in ornamental band, part of lettering incused and part relief. *Rev.* Value and date, wreath.

ALEXANDER III., 1881– 1, 2, 3, and 5 Kopecks as last.

THE KINGDOM OF POLAND.

Once a great European power, now crushed and divided between Russia, Germany, and Austria. The Arms consist of an Eagle quartered with a galloping horseman, sometimes the Eagle alone. The inscriptions are always in *Latin* and easily readable. The following are the coins of the later rulers :—

JOHN CASIMIR.—1648–68, "Solidus." *Obv.* Bust and *ins.* or I.CR. *Rev.* An eagle.

AUGUSTUS III.—1733–63, 1 and 3 "Schillings." *Obv.* Bust and *ins.* *Rev.* Arms and EL SAX. with date.

FIG. 113.—One Schilling of Augustus III., King of Poland and Elector of Saxony.

STANISLAUS-AUGUSTUS.—1764–94, ½, 1, and 3 "Grossus" and "Solidus." *Obv.* "*S.A.R.*" *script monogram* or Bust. *Rev.* Arms or *ins.*

FRED'K AUGUSTUS.—1807–14, 1 and 3 "Grosze." *Obv.* Arms. *Rev.* Value, etc.

ALEXANDER I. (of Russia).—1815–25, 1 and 3 "Grosze," same.

NICHOLAS I.—1825–55, 1 and 3 "Grosze" (varieties). *Obv.* Arms. *Rev.* Value, etc.

RUSSIAN DEPENDENCIES.

LITHUANIA.—"Solidus" of John Casimir (King of Poland), 1660–67. *Obv.* Bust. *Rev.* A horseman.

FINLAND.—Alexander II. (of Russia), 1866–76. 1, 5,

and 10 " Pennia." *Obv. Script "A."* crowned. *Rev.* Value and date.

MOLDAVIA AND WALLACHIA.—Catherine II. (of Russia), 1771–4. 1, 2, and 5 " Paras." *Obv.* Arms, in two oval shields (a steer's head and dove with olive branch) crowned. *Rev.* Value in Greek and Russian.

ROUMANIA.

Only copper coins so far, of King Charles I., 1866–
1*st series*, 1867, pieces of 1, 2, 5, and 10 " Bani," bearing on

FIG. 114.—Ten Bani of Roumania, 1867.

Obv. crowned Arms and the word ROMANIA. *Rev.* Value and date.

2*nd series*, 1879–81, 2 and 5 " Bani." *Obv.* Bust and CAROL I DOMNUL AL ROMANIEI. *Rev.* Arms, value, and date.

3*rd series*, 1882–5, similar, with CAROL I REGE AL ROMANIEI *Rev.* As before.

SERVIA.

MICHAEL III.—1860–79, 1, 5, and 10 " Paras." *Obv.* Head. *Rev.* Value, inscription, etc., Russian characters.

MILAN OBRENOVITCH IV.—1879–89, 5 and 10 " Paras," similar character.

BULGARIA.

1881.—2, 5, and 10 "Stotinki." *Obv.* Arms. *Rev.* Value.

GREECE.

The coinage of modern Greece is a sad departure from the splendour of her ancient prestige in all that pertains to the medallic art. Of course, speaking of later days, her moneys up to 1492 were those of the Byzantine Empire, of which she formed a part. For three centuries, however, the miserable currency of Hellas bore the stamp of the Grand Turk. On her liberation and the organization of a government in 1828, under Count Capo d'Istria, a series of 1, 5, 10, and 20

FIG. 115.—Ten Lepta of Count Capo d'Istria.

"Lepta" was struck of the following pattern: *Obv.* A Phoenix in the midst of flames kindled by a ray from above; over its head the symbol of the cross. Inscription surrounding ΕΛΛΗΝΙΚΗ ΠΟΛΙΤΕΙΑ (the Greek people), mint mark, αωχα, below. *Rev.* value in ΛΕΠΤΑ (Lepta) within a wreath, surrounding ΚΥΒΕΡΝΗΤΗΣ Ι. Α. ΚΑΠΟΔΙΣΤΡΙΑΣ (the Government of J. A. Capo d'Istria) and date. There are three varieties of coins of this same type between 1828 and 1831.

Of King OTHO, 1833–57 (–62) there is a series of 1, 2, 5, and 10 Lepta. *Obv.* Greek cross upon a crowned shield surrounded by ΒΑΣΙΛΕΙΑ ΤΗΣ ΕΛΛΑΔΟΣ (kingdom of the Hellenes). *Rev.* Value in wreath.

Fig. 116.—Ten Lepta, Otho of Greece.

George I., 1869-   .—1, 2, 5, and 10 Lepta.   Type the
same except in some changes in size of lettering and the king

Fig¹ 117.—Five Lepta of King George of Greece.

wearing a moustache after 1878.   *Obv.* Head surrounded by
ΓΕΩΡΓΙΟΣ Α! ΒΑΣΙΛΕΥΣ ΤΩΝ ΕΛΛΗΝΩΝ, date below.   *Rev.* Value
in wreath.

TURKEY.

It is merely necessary to state that the coinage of Turkey is divided according to so many systems as to result in none at all. The coins of this country have been altered as many as thirty-five times in a single reign. Many of the coins issued in the provinces are not current at Constantinople or elsewhere out of their own locality. The types are uniform. *Obv.* The *Toghra* or Imperial cipher, accompanied on Turkish coins

FIG. 118.—Ten Paras of Abdul Medjid.

proper (Constantinople) by a small rose branch, without which they are provincial issues or Egyptian. The *Rev.* have a long circular inscription in native characters, in the centre of which is the value. The latter are usually 1, 5, 10, 20, and 40 Paras. The most common now are of Abdul Medjid, Abdul Aziz, and Abdul Hamid Khan II.

VENETIAN DEPENDENCIES.

Pieces of 1 Soldo and Gazzetta were struck during the sixteenth and part of the seventeenth century for several places. They bear uniformly the lion of St. Mark on *Obv.*, usually surrounded by s. MARC. VEN. The *Rev.* generally gives the locality, with or without value, sometimes value alone. These coins will be found of ARMATA and MOREA combined, DALMA(tia) and ALBAN(ia) combined, ISOLE and ARMAT(a) combined, and CORFU, CEF(alonia), and ZAN(te) combined. Of CANDIA some of the coins bear value of 1 or $2\frac{1}{2}$ SOLDINI, others in "Tornesi," with a Greek inscription.

CYPRUS.

A few mediæval copper coins exist, such as a " Cavallo " of the fourteenth century kings, and later coins of Venetian origin, with the Lion of St. Mark.   In 1879 a British colonial series was issued (see "Colonial Coins and Tokens ").

MALTA.

Copper coins were issued by the Grand Masters from a very early date.   It is not necessary to go into minute details, because certain general types continue through all the long series.   The principal are as follows—1. Two hands clasped.

FIG. 119.—Ten Grains.   Alofius de Wignacourt, Grand Master.

2. Head of John the Baptist on a plate, *ins.* usually NON AES SED FIDES.   3. A Maltese cross, with *ins.* IN HOC SIGNO MILITAMUS, date in angles of cross.   The Arms of Malta are generally the personal Arms of the Grand Master quartered with a St. George's cross on a crowned shield.   The values in copper

FIG. 120.—One Grain.   Adrian de Wignacourt, Grand Master.

are : "Picciolo," v, x, and xx "Tari," and I, v, x, or xx "Grani."   The coins of each Grand Master will be easily identified by his name and arms.

Claude de la Sengle, 1553-7.—Five scallops on a St. Andrew's cross.

John de la Valette-Parisot, 1557–68.—A Falcon and Lion *rampant*.

Peter del Monte, 1568–72.—Three Mountains on a diagonal bar.

John de la Cassiere, 1572–81.—A Lion *rampant*.

Hugo de Loubens Verdalle, 1582–95.—A Wolf *rampant*.

Martin Garzes, 1596–1601.—A Swan.

Alofius de Wignacourt, 1601–22.—Three *fleur de lis* under a label.

Louis Mendez de Vasconcellos, 1622–23.—Three indented bars.

Anton de Paula, 1623–36.—A Peacock.

John Paul Lascaris Castellar, 1636–57.—A double-headed Eagle.

FIG. 121.—Four Tari of John Paul Lascaris Castellar, Grand Master (Counterstamped.)

Adrian de Wignacourt, 1690–97.—Three *fleur de lis*.

Raimond Perellos-Roccaful, 1697–1720.—Three Pears.

Anton Manoel de Vilhena, 1722–35.—Lion *rampant*, or winged hand holding sword.

Raimund Despuig.—1736–41, A Star upon a peak, *fleur de lis* above.

Emanuel Pinto de Fonseca, 1741–73.—Five Crescents

Emanuel de Rohan, 1775–97.—Nine Diamonds.

Butler & Tanner, The Selwood Printing Works, Frome, and London.

SPINK & SON LTD.

are the Publishers of the following

STANDARD WORKS

HANDBOOK OF THE COINS OF GREAT BRITAIN & IRELAND IN THE BRITISH MUSEUM. Revised 1970 by Dr. J. P. C. Kent, I. H. Stewart, P. Finn and H. W. A. Linecar £7

THE DATING AND ARRANGEMENT OF THE UNDATED COINS OF ROME, A.D. 98–148. By Dr. P. V. Hill. 1970 £6

THE NORMAN CONQUEST AND THE ENGLISH COINAGE. By Michael Dolley 80p

LATE ROMAN BRONZE COINAGE, A.D. 324–498. By P. V. Hill, R. A. G. Carson and J. P. C. Kent. New impression 1972. £4

ATLAS DE MONNAIES GAULOISES. By H. de la Tour. Reprint of the 1892 edition, with new map £8

THE MILLED COINAGE OF ENGLAND. Edited by Howard Linecar £3

COINS & MEDALS OF THE KNIGHTS OF MALTA. By H. C. Schembri. Reprint of the 1908 edition in a more handy size £6

THE COINAGE OF ANCIENT BRITAIN. By R. P. Mack. Third edition £5

ENGLISH HAMMERED COINAGE. 2 vols. By J. J. North. Vol. 1 £5
Vol. 2 second edition £8

THE COINAGES OF EDWARD I & II. By J. J. North. 1968 80p

RUSSIAN GOLD COINS. By E. E. Clain-Stefanelli £1

THE STANDARD CATALOGUE OF BRITISH ORDERS, DECORATIONS & MEDALS. By E. C. Joslin. Third edition. 1976. Cloth. Coloured plates. £5·50

THE COINS OF THE BRITISH COMMONWEALTH OF NATIONS TO THE END OF THE REIGN OF GEORGE VI. By Major F. Pridmore
Part 1. Europe £5
Part 2. Asia excluding India. To be reprinted
Part 3. The West Indies. With valuations £8
Part 4. India. Vol. 1. E.I.C. £30

COINS AND COINAGES OF THE STRAITS SETTLEMENTS AND BRITISH MALAYA, 1786–1951. By Major F. Pridmore £3

EUROPEAN CROWNS AND TALERS SINCE 1800. By J. S. Davenport £6

A MANUAL OF ANGLO-GALLIC GOLD COINS. By R. D. Beresford-Jones £3

HISTORIA NUMORUM. By Barclay V. Head. 1911 edition reprinted £15

GREEK COINS AND CITIES. By Norman Davis. 1967 £5

ENGLISH PROOF AND PATTERN CROWN SIZE PIECES, 1658–1960. By H. W. A. Linecar and A. G. Stone £5

THE SCOTTISH COINAGE. By I. H. Stewart. 1967. £3

MEDALLIC ILLUSTRATIONS OF THE HISTORY OF GREAT BRITAIN AND IRELAND. By E. Hawkins £15

HISTORICAL REFERENCES ON COINS OF THE ROMAN EMPIRE. By E. A. Sydenham £3

THE GUIDE BOOK TO THE COINAGE OF IRELAND. By A. Dowle and P. Finn £2

BANKNOTES AND BANKING IN THE ISLE OF MAN. By E. Quarmby £3

CHINESE CASH. By O. D. Cresswell £1·50

THE HISTORY OF THE ORDER OF THE BATH & ITS INSIGNIA. By J. C. Risk £5
De Luxe numbered edition of 150 £12·50

BRITISH BATTLES AND MEDALS. By Major L. L. Gordon. 4th edition, revised by E. C. Joslin £10

CATALOGUE OF ALEXANDRIAN COINS. By J. G. Milne. Reprinted with supplement 1971 £6

THE BATH MINT. By L. V. Grinsell 90p

MEDIEVAL ENGLISH JETONS. By G. Berry £3

DICTIONARY OF NUMISMATIC NAMES. By A. R. Frey £6

BRITISH COUNTERMARKS ON COPPER AND BRONZE COINS. By J. Gavin Scott £8·50

M.G.S. 1793–1814. CANADIAN RECIPIENTS. By Miss B. Wilson £8

SPANISH DOLLARS & SILVER TOKENS. By E. M. Kelly £8